Skills for Better Reading
< Intermediate >
— Third Edition —

構造で読む英文エッセイ〈中級編〉

【第３版】

Yumiko Ishitani

NAN'UN-DO

Download Audio

音声ファイル
無料 DL
のご案内

このテキストの音声を無料で視聴（ストリーミング）・ダウンロードできます。自習用音声としてご活用ください。
以下のサイトにアクセスしてテキスト番号で検索してください。

https://nanun-do.com　テキスト番号［**512101**］

※ 無線 LAN（WiFi）に接続してのご利用を推奨いたします。

※ 音声ダウンロードは Zip ファイルでの提供になります。
お使いの機器によっては別途ソフトウェア（アプリケーション）の導入が必要となります。

Read by
Karen Haedrich
Chris Koprowski

※ SKills for Better Reading <Intermediate> 音声ダウンロードページは以下の QR コードからもご利用になれます。

Skills for Better Reading
＜Intermediate＞
—Third Edition—

1 構造で読む英文エッセイ

本書の目的は、「全体的なエッセイ構造を考えながら内容を掴む」ということを体得することにあります。そうすることによって、少し内容の難しい英文でも速く読むことができるはずです。英文においては、それぞれのエッセイにはそれぞれ目的があり、論理によって進んでいく、ということが、日本文よりも明確です。それぞれのパラグラフに役割があり、その組み合わせで、ひとつの目的に向かって進んでいるということを掴んでください。本書ではそれぞれのパラグラフがどのような役割をもっているのかに重点を置いて作られています。４つの典型的なエッセイ構造を提示しておりますが、この基本を身につけることによって、次にどのような内容のパラグラフがくるのか、筆者がどういう方向に行こうとしているのかを推測する力がついてくるはずです。

もちろん、新聞・雑誌の英文では、こうした基本的パターンをさまざまに変化させたものが使われています。本書では、４段落でひとつのまとまりが基本ですが、実際にはその他にさまざまな役割をもった段落が差し挟まれているのが通常です。または基本４段落の中のひと段落がいくつかの段落に分けられていることが実際にはほとんどです。そのことをふまえた上で、それでも根底を流れている基本パターンを掴むことは内容理解には非常に大切なことだと思います。本書を作成する上で、英文チェックなどChristofer Bullsmith氏には大変お世話になりました。ここに感謝いたします。

2 本書の使い方

本書はそれぞれの課が４ページ構成になっています。

1 第１ページで、エッセイのおおまかな構造を掴んでください。ひとつのエッセイがどういう流れで構成されているのかに着目してください。

2 第２ページで、そこで取り扱われる構成パターンを使った読みもの（Reading A）があります。テーマになっている構造を頭に入れながら読んでください。

3 第３ページでは、問題を解くことでReading Aの内容確認を行います。１の問題で、それぞれの段落からの問題を日本語で出しています。日本語を介してそのエッセイの内容が頭に入っているかを確認します。2-4の問題は英語による内容確認問題です。真偽問題、マッチング問題、要約を完成させる問題、定義にあてはまる単語を本文から探すもの、などです。日本語である程度内容を確認したら、あとは英語に頭を切り替えて、できるだけたくさんの英語に触れてください。

4 第４ページは、もうひとつの読み物、Reading Bです。こちらも、その課でテーマになっているエッセイ構造となっています。Reading Aよりも短く、簡単になっておりますので、わからない単語も無視して、一気に読んで内容が頭に入ってくるか試してください。それぞれのエッセイに、それぞれのパラグラフを簡単に日本語でまとめる作業を付しておきました。テーマとなる構造を定着させてください。

本書はあくまでも、全体的な内容を掴むということを目的にしております。細かいところを気にせずに、パラグラフのポイント、ポイントを素早く掴むということに重きを置いております。もちろんさらにReading力をつけるためには、精読も必要ですので、あとで英文の細かな分析を行うこともお勧めいたします。

3　ここで扱う４つのエッセイパターン

このテキストでは、エッセイのパターンを次の４つの型に分けています。

1. 意見サポート型
2. パラグラフ並列型
3. 直線型
4. 異質パラグラフ型

それぞれのパラグラフそれぞれのエッセイの中でどのような役割を果たすかということについて、簡単に図示してあります。

◎ 第１のパターン：意見サポート型

Unit 1 ～ 3

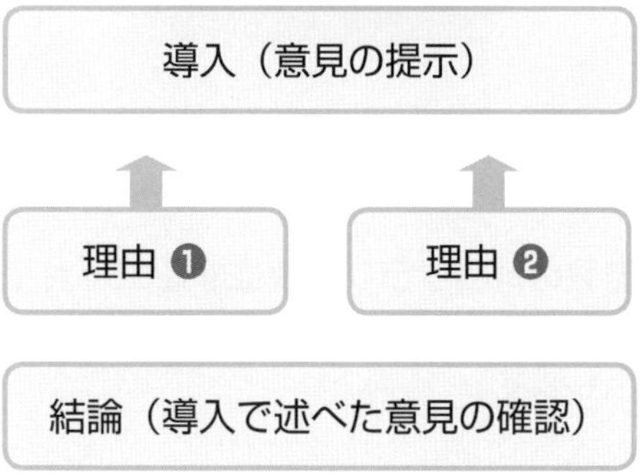

最初に自分の意見を明確にし、それを支える理由をその後の段落で述べていくパターン。最後の段落では最初に述べた意見をもう一度確認します。このテキストでは、①～③課で次の３種類を提示します。

① 結論・理由
② 社会事象の説明
③ 結果・原因

◎ 第２のパターン：パラグラフ並列型

Unit 4 ～ 7

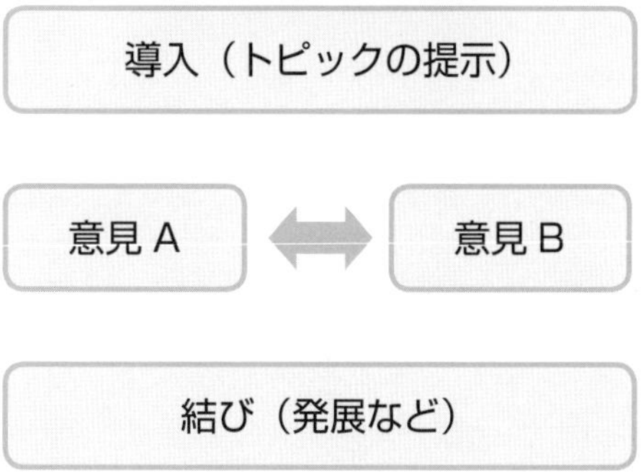

トピックを説明するいくつかのパラグラフがそれぞれ同じ重要性をもって並列に配置されるエッセイパターンです。このテキストでは、④～⑦課で次の４種類を提示します。

④ 複数の意見
⑤ 比較
⑥ 賛成・反対
⑦ 分類

◎ 第３のパターン：直線型

Unit 8 ～ 10

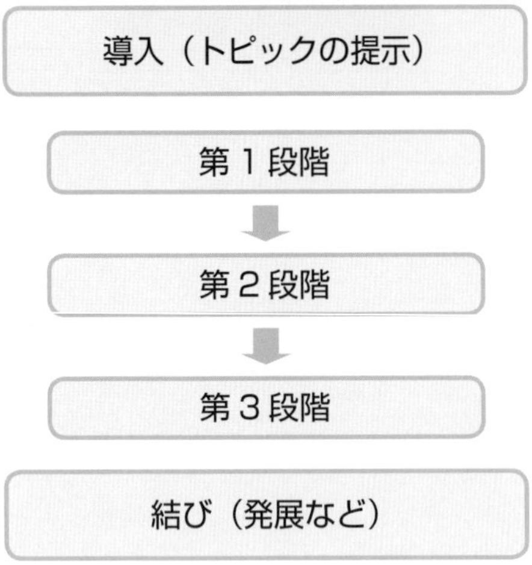

時間の流れに沿って順に説明をしていくものです。このテキストでは、⑧～⑩課で次の３種類を提示します。

⑧ **歴史**
⑨ **過程**
⑩ **原因ー結果**

◎ 第４のパターン：異質パラグラフ型

Unit 11 ～ 14

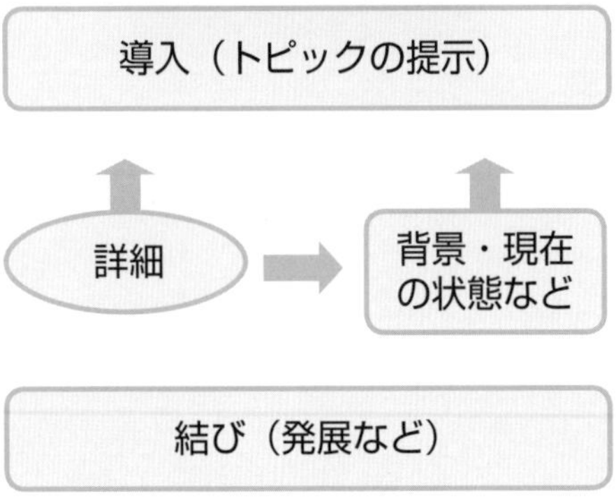

役割の違う複数のパラグラフで構成するエッセイパターンです。このテキストでは⑩～⑭課で次の４種類を提示します。

⑪ **問題解決**
⑫ **言葉の定義**
⑬ **実験**
⑭ **新製品**

Contents

Part I

第１のパターン：意見サポート型

（Unit 1 ～ 3）

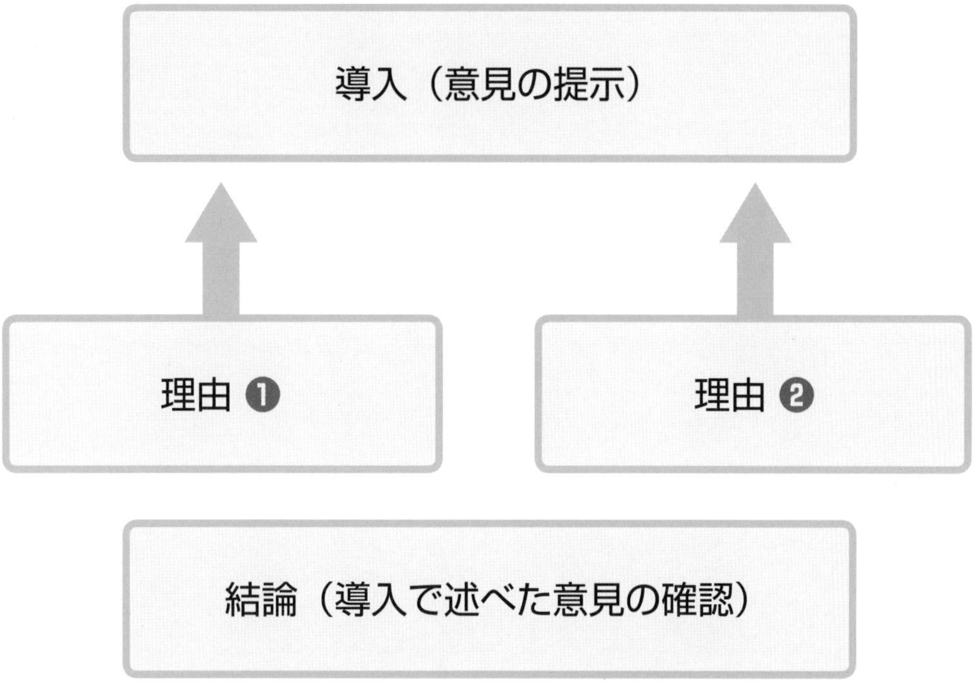

最初に自分の意見を明確にし、それを支える理由をその後の段落で述べていくパターン。最後の段落では最初に述べた意見をもう一度確認します。このテキストでは、①～③課で次の３種類を提示します。

① 結論・理由
② 社会事象の説明
③ 結果・原因

Part I

1 Conclusions / Reasons
理由で押し切る！

エッセイ構成

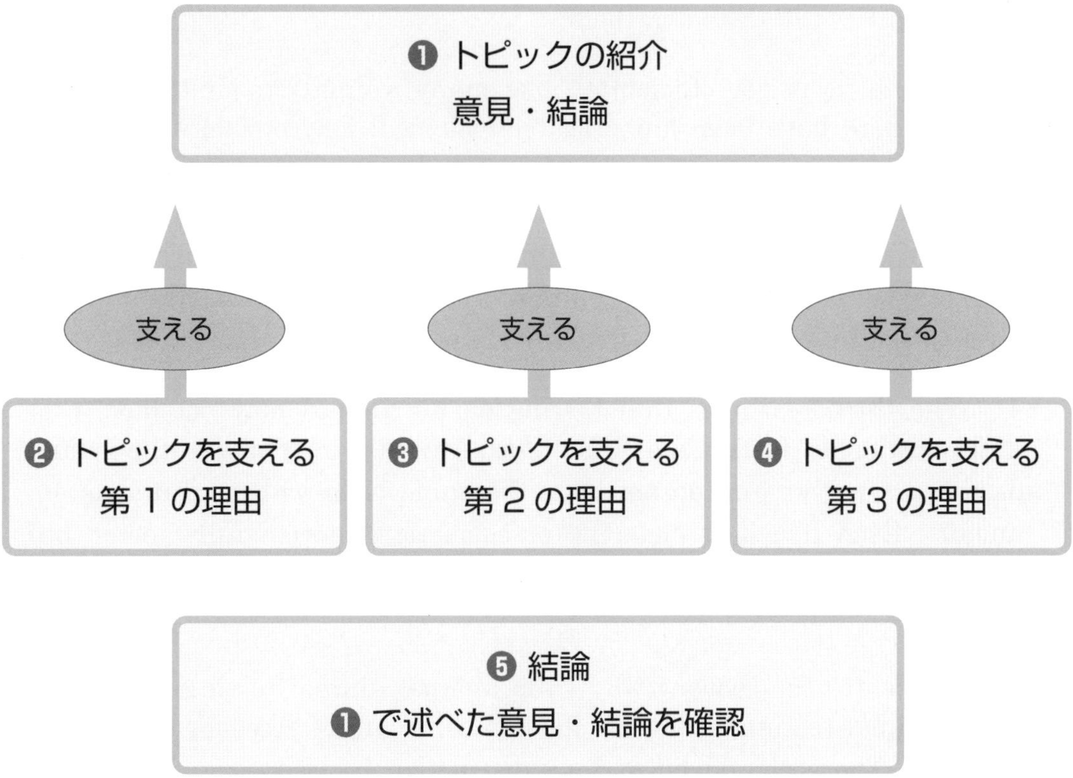

論議を読んでいる問題について、自分はそれについて「賛成だ」または「反対だ」として自分の意見を明確にして、それを正当化するために、いくつかの理由を出し、最後に「こういうわけで自分はこの結論に達した」と締めるエッセイです。

A Should animal testing be allowed?

1 Many people believe animal testing is necessary in order to develop new medicines or cosmetics. Some say that without these tests, we cannot know how the medicine will work. However, I am against animal testing.

2 First, it is morally wrong to cause pain and death to animals. Animals have the right to live, in the same way as humans do. They should not have to suffer at human hands. To save one person's life, thousands of animals may be killed. Many animals suffer terrible pain when cosmetics are tested on them.

3 Second, it is not efficient to use many animals to find the same results. There have been amazing technological developments in recent years. For example, we can use computer models instead of testing on animals. Also, thanks to developments in biotechnology, we can use cells instead of the whole body of an animal to carry out tests. Furthermore, we can now easily share information with other scientists around the world on the Internet and can avoid repeating the same experiments.

4 The third reason is that testing on an animal may not have the same results as testing on a human. Animals do not get the same diseases as we do, and do not have the same biological mechanisms as humans. Even if a new medicine or cosmetic is successfully tested on an animal, it does not mean it will work in the same way on the human body.

5 These are the reasons why I am against animal testing. Even if I accept animal testing to develop medicines, I cannot accept it to develop cosmetics. There should be a clear distinction between saving people's lives and just making women look a little more beautiful.

1 それぞれの段落について、次の質問に答えなさい。

1. 動物実験に対する筆者の結論は？

____

2. 筆者の結論の第一の理由は？

____

3. 筆者の結論の第二の理由は？

____

4. 筆者の結論の第三の理由は？

____

5. 筆者は動物実験の際にはどういう区別をつけるべきであると言っているか？

____

2 Write "T" if the statement is true and "F" if the statement is false.

(　) 1. Animals have the right to live.
(　) 2. Computers will make scientists do more animal testing.
(　) 3. Animal testing is necessary for the development of both medicine and cosmetics.
(　) 4. The whole body of an animal is necessary for animal testing.
(　) 5. We don't need so many animals for animal testing thanks to the spread of the Internet.
(　) 6. An animal's body is different from a human body.
(　) 7. The development of medicine is more important than that of cosmetics.

3 Which statement (A-C) in the box is each of the following statements linked to?

(　) 1. The same medicine can have different effects on animals.
(　) 2. Scientists can share information with each other.
(　) 3. We don't need to kill an animal because we may need just a cell from it.
(　) 4. Computer models can be used instead of animals.
(　) 5. Animals have the right to live.
(　) 6. Many animals are killed to save one person's life.

A. Animal testing is morally wrong.
B. We can carry out animal testing more efficiently.
C. Human bodies and animals' bodies are different.

Notes

1 develop 開発する　cosmetics 化粧品　2 morally 道義的に　at human hands 人間の手で
3 efficient 効率的な　cell 細胞　carry out 行う　furthermore さらに　share 共有する　avoid 避ける
4 disease 病気　mechanism 機構・メカニズム　work on ～に働く　5 accept 受け入れる
distinction 区別

B Should nuclear power plants be abolished in Japan?

1 The terrible Higashi-Nihon Earthquake in 2011 has heated up the discussion over Japan's use of nuclear power. It is true nuclear power is "clean" and powerful, compared with fossil fuels. However, I am still against the use of nuclear power in Japan.

2 The first reason is Japan's geographic situation. Japan has suffered from many earthquakes throughout its history. It is very dangerous if a nuclear plant is hit by a natural disaster like an earthquake.

3 The second reason is that Japan has technology, and has the ability to develop much safer energy than nuclear energy. This would be a good chance for Japan to lead the world by developing cleaner and safer energy for the future.

4 The third reason is that Japan could lead the world in terms of nuclear issues, telling other people how dangerous nuclear power is. Japan is the only country which has experienced atomic bombs. Japan could use these experiences to campaign against nuclear power.

5 For these reasons, I am against the use of nuclear power in Japan. By ending nuclear power, we could change the course of history.

上の文章の内容をまとめてみよう。

① 導入：筆者の意見

② 理由１

③ 理由２

④ 理由３

⑤ 結論

Notes

nuclear power plant 原子力発電所 abolish 廃止する 1 heat up a discussion 議論を白熱させる compared with ～と比べて fossil fuel 化石燃料 2 geographic 地理的な disaster 災害 4 dangerous 危険な atomic bomb 原爆 campaign against ～に反対運動を行う 5 end 終わらせる course 流れ

Part I

2 Social Trends
社会事象を考える

エッセイ構成

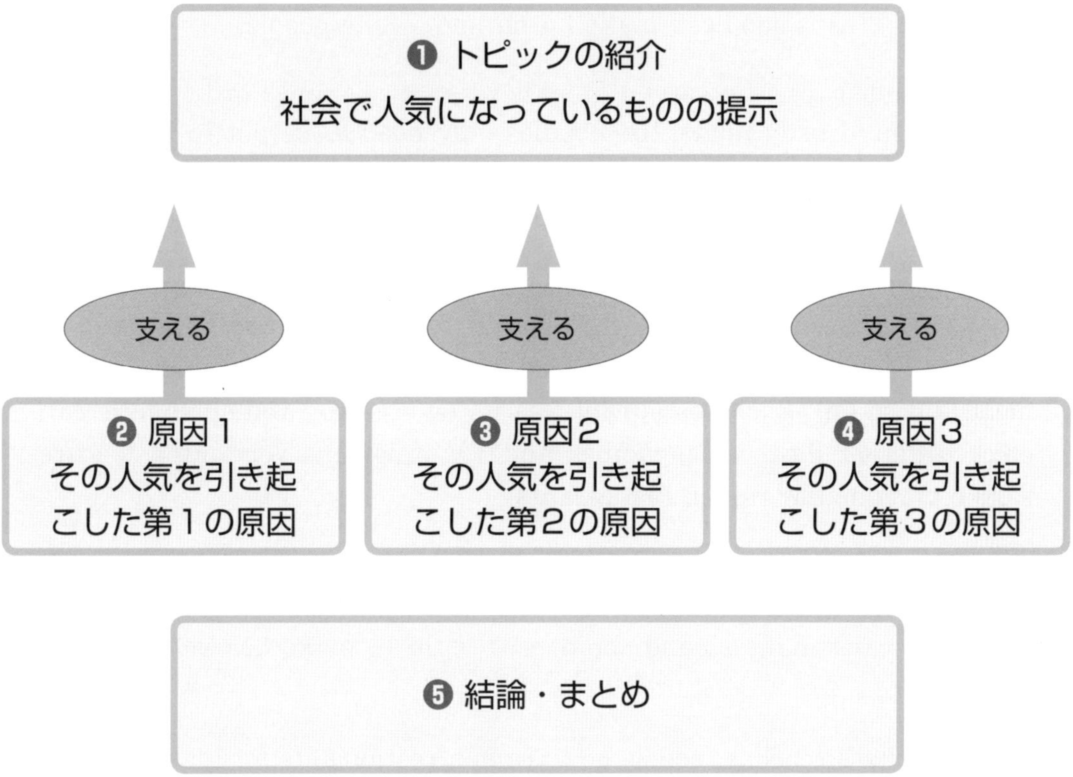

トピックとなる社会事象を紹介し、その事象が現れた社会的原因・背景をいくつか提示していくパターンです。それぞれあげる原因が、トピックを説明し、支える構成となっています。

A Ramen

1 Some people say that ramen is one of Japan's national dishes, along with sushi and tempura. It was originally a Chinese dish, but the Japanese changed it in their way. Now, people are queuing in front of popular ramen restaurants. Why do Japanese people like ramen?

2 The first reason is that it is "all in one." This means that all the ingredients are in one bowl. It is oily, but very nutritious because a lot of toppings are on it, such as vegetables, seaweed and meat. The soup is also nutritious. This is good especially for hungry young people.

3 Second, it can be served quickly after a customer orders, because the broth is already made, the noodles only need to be put in hot water, and the toppings are already prepared. A cook just puts these ingredients into a bowl. It takes very little time both to serve ramen and to eat it.

4 The third reason is that there are many variations, such as the broth (meat-based, fish-based, miso-based, shoyu-based, etc.), the noodles (straight, curly, thin, thick etc.) and the toppings (various vegetables, meat and so on). Each restaurant has its own recipe and customers can enjoy different flavors. Magazines and TV programs very often feature ramen and popular ramen restaurants.

5 The fourth reason is that you cannot make ramen easily at home. It takes a long time to make the broth, sometimes a whole day. An ordinary housewife can't make it, and she doesn't want to make her kitchen dirty with oil.

6 For these reasons, people go to ramen restaurants for lunch. It is so delicious and convenient that they don't mind waiting in a line.

1 それぞれの段落について、次の質問に答えなさい。

1. ラーメンの歴史を簡潔に述べよ。

___

2. ラーメンが人気の第一の理由とは？

___

3. ラーメンが人気の第二の理由とは？

___

4. ラーメンが人気の第三の理由とは？

___

5. ラーメンが人気の第四の理由とは？

___

6. 人々がランチにラーメンを食べる 2 つの理由を挙げよ。

 1. ___
 2. ___

2 Write "T" if the statement is true and "F" if the statement is false.

(　　) 1. It is easy to make ramen and even children can do it.

(　　) 2. Housewives often go to ramen restaurants because there are many restaurants which serve special ramen for housewives.

(　　) 3. Ramen contains a variety of ingredients, so it is nutritious.

(　　) 4. When you are busy, ramen is a good choice, because it is served almost immediately after you order.

(　　) 5. Shoyu-based broth is the best of all broth flavors.

(　　) 6. Media feature ramen very often.

3 Fill in the blanks to complete the following summary.

Ramen is originally a ([1] 　　　　) dish but the ([2] 　　　　) changed it into their own style. It is very popular because many ([3] 　　　　) are in it, it is served quickly, it has many ([4] 　　　　) and it is hard to make it at ([5] 　　　　).

4 Find the word in the text with the same meaning as the statement.

1. a very thin, long strip of pasta or similar flour paste, eaten with a sauce or in a soup (n 　　　　)
2. a person who buys goods or service from a shop or business (c 　　　　)
3. a round, deep dish or basin used for food or liquid (b 　　　　)

Notes

[1] along with ～と並んで　originally 元々　queue 列をなす　[2] ingredient 材料
nutritious 栄養のある　topping（上にのせる）具　[3] broth だし・スープ　[4] variation 種類
curly ちぢれた　recipe レシピ・調理法　flavor 風味　feature ～を特集する　[5] ordinary 普通の
housewife 主婦

B Cat cafés

1 The name "cat café" ("neko café" in Japanese) appeared in Japan in 2005. Now there are many cat cafés in Japan. A cat café is a theme café where customers watch and play with cats while drinking a cup of coffee. Why are these cafés so popular in Japan?

2 The main reason is the lack of space to keep a pet at home. Cat cafés are popular mainly in cities where most people live in apartments. In many apartments, pets are not allowed, because of the smell, noise and so on.

3 The second reason is that many people are allergic to animal hairs. Children are especially sensitive to house dust, including animal hairs. Not only children but also adults are afraid of developing allergies. Even if you love cats, you can't keep one if somebody in your family is allergic to animal hairs.

4 For these reasons, people go to cat cafés instead of keeping pets at home. Other pet cafés have appeared these days, such as "rabbit cafés" or "dog cafés."

上の文章の内容をまとめてみよう。

① 導入 → ② 理由1

③ 理由2 → ④ 結論

Notes

1 a theme café テーマ・カフェ　2 lack 不足　allow 許す　3 be allergic to ～にアレルギーがある
be sensitive to ～に敏感である　including ～を含めて　allergy アレルギー

Part I

3 Results / Causes
原因を究明する

エッセイ構成

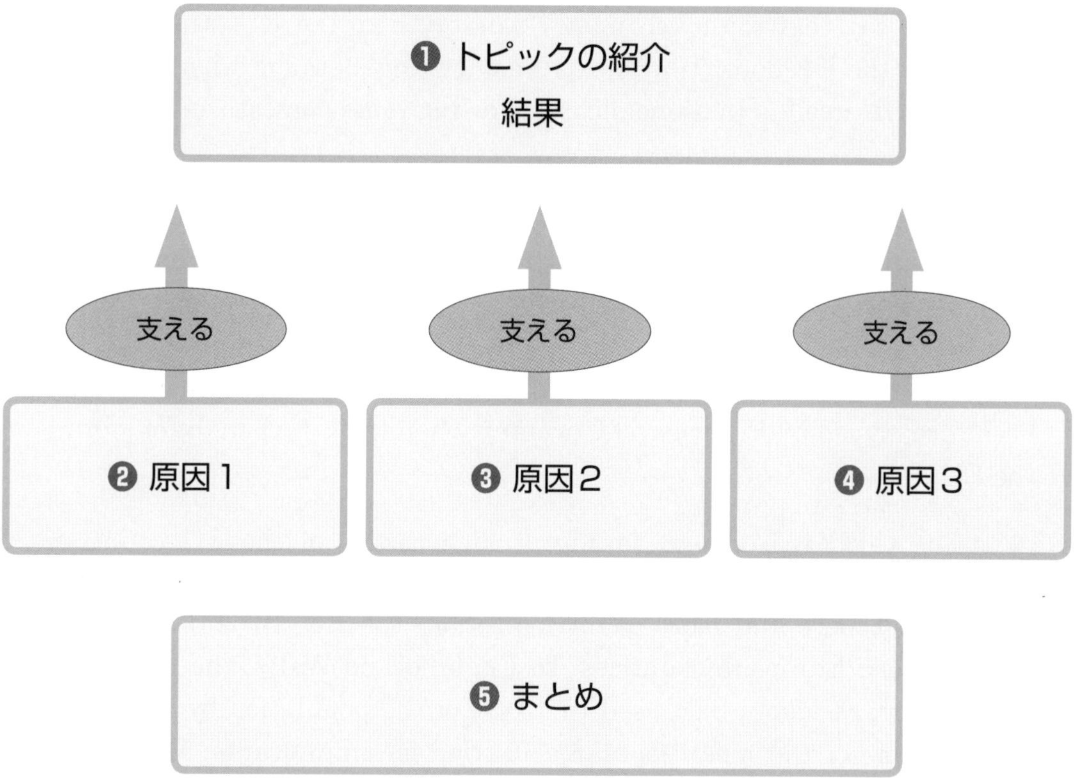

現在起こっている事象、最近のニュースを結果ととらえ、なぜその結果が引き起こされたのか、その原因が述べられているエッセイです。

A Why did the UK choose to leave the EU?

1 On 23 June 2016, the UK decided to leave the EU as a result of a national referendum, which surprised the world. 52% voted to leave and 48% voted to stay. The UK was the second biggest economic member in the EU, so the impact on the EU is huge. Why did the UK vote to leave the EU?

2 The first reason was money. As the second biggest economic member, the UK had to support other poorer members of the EU. Some politicians say that too much money was given to the EU. Many people think that the UK doesn't have extra money any more for other countries when the UK itself is in economic crisis owing to its domestic issues.

3 The second reason was the UK's political independence. As a member of the EU, the UK had to obey the European parliament and court. Many felt that the UK could not decide many issues themselves. Even after joining the EU, the UK never accepted the euro as its currency and kept their own currency, the pound. From the beginning, the UK hesitated to join the EU for this political reason, because the EU had been already led by France and Germany when the UK thought of joining the EU.

4 The third reason was immigration. Citizens of the EU countries have the right to travel, live and work anywhere inside the EU. The EU allowed more and more countries to join the EU. In 2004, it added eight eastern European countries. In England and Wales, the number of foreign-born residents increased to 13.4% of the population by 2011. The UK was one of the most popular countries for immigrants. Because of increased immigration, the UK's economic burden became huge.

5 Thus the UK finally left the EU in 2020. It will be very interesting to see how the UK will manage their relationship with the EU in the future.

1 それぞれの段落について、次の質問に答えなさい。

1. イギリスはEUでどのくらい重要な国であったか？

____

2. イギリスのEUにおける経済問題とは何か？

____

3. イギリスは貨幣についてどういう政策をとったか？

____

4. 移民の増大でイギリスはどんな問題を抱えていたか？

____

5. イギリスがEUから独立したのはいつか？

____

2 Fill in the blanks.

1. 48 percent of British people said "([1])" to the EU, while 52 percent said "No" in the national referendum.
2. The UK was the ([2]) biggest economic country in the EU.
3. The UK has refused to accept the ([3]) and continued to use the ([4]) as their currency.
4. Under EU, the UK had to accept many ([5]) from other EU members.

3 Answer the following questions in English.

1. What method did the UK choose to decide whether they should leave the EU or not?

____

2. How many countries were there in the EU which were economically bigger than the UK?

____

Notes

[1] national referendum 国民投票　vote to V ～することに投票する　impact on ～に及ぼす衝撃
[2] domestic issues 国内問題　[3] independence 独立　obey 従う　parliament 議会　court 裁判所
issue 問題　currency 通貨　[4] immigration 移民　add 加える　foreign-born 外国生まれの
resident 住民　burden 負担　[5] thus このようにして　manage ～を扱う

B Why are more and more people suffering from pollen allergies?

1 Pollen allergies occur when the immune system overreacts to pollen in the air. Pollen allergy is not a new disease, but now there are more and more people suffering from it. Why?

2 First, there are more chemicals in the air. They come from cars and factories, and the amount is increasing. These chemicals are mixed with pollen and are causing pollen allergies.

3 Second, the streets are now covered with asphalt. In the past, pollen fell on the ground and was absorbed by it, but pollen is not absorbed by the asphalt. Pollen stays in the air.

4 Third, people live in clean houses. In the past, many people lived on farms and they were breathing in animal hair. Many people lived in big families in dirty houses, so they were used to dust. Now, the environment is kept clean and people are not used to breathing in dust.

5 Pollen allergy is a modern and urban disease. If we continue to live in cities, we have to cope with pollen allergies.

上の文章の内容をまとめてみよう。

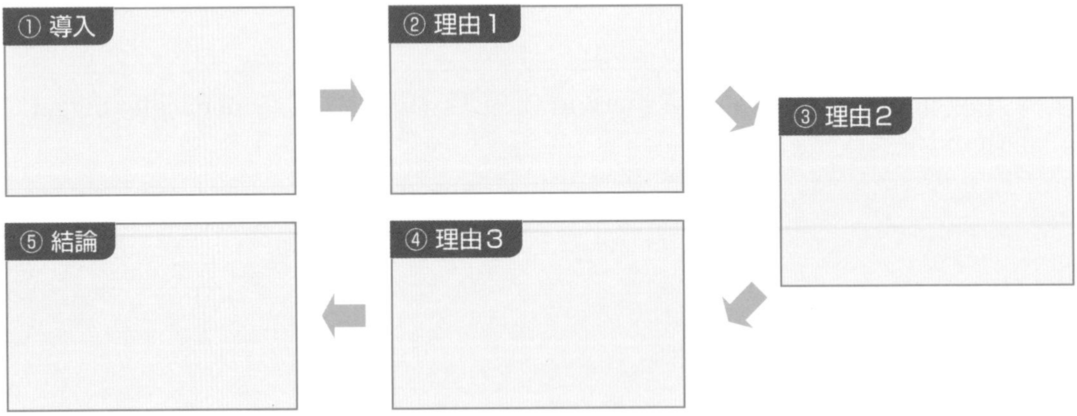

Notes

pollen allergy 花粉症　1 the immune system 免疫系　overreact 過度に反応する　2 chemical 化学物質　3 asphalt アスファルト　absorb 吸収する　4 breathe in ～を吸い込む　be used to ～に慣れてい　5 urban 都市の

Part II

第2のパターン：パラグラフ並列型

（Unit 4 〜 7）

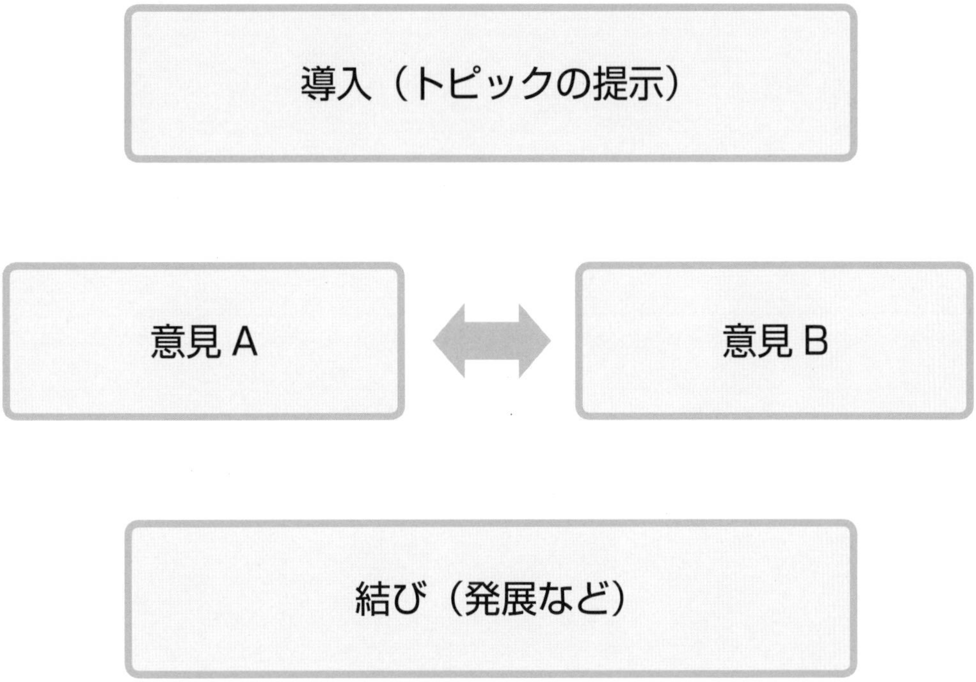

トピックを説明するいくつかのパラグラフがそれぞれ同じ重要性をもって並列に配置されるエッセイパターンです。このテキストでは、④〜⑦課で次の４種類を提示します。

④ 複数の意見
⑤ 比較
⑥ 賛成・反対
⑦ 分類

Part II

4 Several Explanations
いくつかの説明

エッセイ構成

なにかの不思議な自然現象、社会現象、歴史的出来事を提示し、なぜその現象が起きたのか、いくつかの可能性のある説明を紹介するエッセイパターンです。

A Crop circles

1 Have you heard of "crop circles"? If you hear that this means "mystery circles," you may say yes, because this phrase has appeared on TV or in magazines for a long time. Strange circles have been found in fields for centuries. These circles are called "crop circles." They are called "mystery circles" in Japan. The question is who created such a complicated pattern. There are several explanations.

2 The first explanation seems ridiculous. Some people say they are the work of UFOs. They believe that crop circles are the work of visitors from other planets. Some people claim that they saw UFO-like lights and heard strange noises from crop circles before they were formed.

3 The second one is more scientific and persuasive. Some people say crop circles are the result of a natural phenomenon. The most scientific explanation is that crop circles are created by swirling winds. Such winds are common in hilly areas such as parts of southern England. Some people say that the earth creates its own energy, which forms the circles. In fact, some scientists found strong magnetic fields inside crop circles.

4 The third explanation is that crop circles are tricks by teams of circlemakers. Small planes or helicopters are used to create patterns, people say. Some news surprised British people and proved this explanation was right. In 1991, two British men announced that they had made hundreds of crop circles since 1978. They said they made circles with a rope and board.

5 It's true that some crop circles proved to be man-made thanks to the confession of those British men. However, there are still many crop circles in the world which can't be explained by just the "man-made" theory. This phenomenon is still a mystery.

1 それぞれの段落について、次の質問に答えなさい。

1. クロップサークル（ミステリーサークル）とは何か？

____

2. どんなものを見聞きしたことが UFO 説を裏付けているか？

____

3. 最も科学的な説明とは何か？

____

4. 誰かのいたずらだとする人々はどんなものが用いられたと言っているか？

____

5.「人工」説を 100%肯定できない理由とは？

____

2 Write "T" if the statement is true and "F" if the statement is false.

(　　) 1. Crop circles are sometimes found in mountains.
(　　) 2. Crop circles are a little different from mystery circles.
(　　) 3. Some people have announced that crop circles were their work.

3 Fill in the blanks.

1. Crop circles are called ([1] 　　　　　　) circles in Japan.
2. UFOs may have created crop circles, because some people saw strange ([2] 　　　　　　) and heard strange ([3] 　　　　　　) from crop circles.
3. Swirling winds are seen very often in ([4] 　　　　　　) areas.
4. Some people found strong ([5] 　　　　　　) fields in crop circles.
5. Two men confessed that they made crop circles using a ([6] 　　　　　　) and ([7] 　　　　　　).

4 Find the word in the text with the same meaning as the statement.

1. a repeated decorative design (　　　　　　)
2. a cunning act to deceive someone (　　　　　　)

Notes

[1] complicated 複雑な　[2] ridiculous ばかげた　[3] persuasive 説得的な　phenomenon 現象　swirling 旋回する　hilly 丘の　form 形成する　magnetic field 磁場　[4] trick いたずら　announce 発表する　board 板　[5] prove to V ～であることがわかる　confession 告白　theory 理論

B Acupuncture

09

1 Acupuncture is a kind of medical treatment in China, Korea, Japan, etc. Needles are used to stimulate certain points on the body in order to relieve pains and heal chronic diseases. Scientists have been studying how it works on the body. Here are some possible explanations.

2 One major theory is that the needle stimulates a nerve. And the nerve sends signals to the brain, and the brain releases neural hormones. Then the patient feels happy and feels less pain.

3 The second explanation is that acupuncture reduces proteins in the body. When the proteins decrease in the body, it decreases inflammation and pain.

4 The third explanation is that by putting the needle in your body, you stimulate the brain to release some nerve growth factor and it helps the nerve to regenerate.

5 Although some scientists doubt the effects of acupuncture on the body it may not be wise to ignore its effects.

上の文章の内容をまとめてみよう。

① 導入 → ② 説明1 → ③ 説明2 → ④ 説明3 → ⑤ まとめ

Notes

acupuncture 鍼《はり》　1 stimulate 刺激する　relieve とり除く　chronic 慢性の　possible 可能性のある
2 nerve 神経　release 出す・分泌する　neural 神経の　hormone ホルモン　patient 患者
3 reduce 減らす　protein タンパク質　inflammation 炎症　4 nerve growth factor 神経成長要素
regenerate 再生する　5 doubt 疑う　ignore 無視する　effect 影響

Part II

5 Comparison
比べてみよう！

エッセイ構成

なにか似ているものや事象をとりあげて比較するエッセイパターン。この課では、比較対象物 A と B をそれぞれ別のパラグラフで説明します。また、何か比較基準に沿って各パラグラフ内で二者を比較して進んでいくパターンもあります。

A Pigeons and doves

1 Do you know the difference between a "pigeon" and a "dove"? The word "pigeon" is originally French, while "dove" comes from the German word "Taube." However, the difference is much deeper than that.

2 A "pigeon" is a bird, usually grey in color, which often lives in towns. You can see it in parks, on the street and in your neighborhood. Sometimes people complain of pigeons because of their noise and nests. Some hate pigeons because they make towns dirty, and sometimes put up signs saying "Don't feed the pigeons". Pigeons were domesticated and sometimes used as messengers (homing pigeons). A Japanese company called "pigeon" sells a baby's feeding bottle. The name is from the fact that a pigeon releases milk-like liquid. A pigeon also means a person who loses money in gambling.

3 A "dove" is a small kind of pigeon that is not domesticated. A dove is white, while a pigeon is grey. An American company selling soap and shampoo is called "Dove" and the name is linked to the whiteness of the dove and its image of peace. Why is a dove linked to peace? The story goes back to the Bible. There was a big flood as a result of God's anger at the corruption of human beings. Noah saved pairs of animals on his ark (ship). After the flood, he released a dove to see whether the flood was over. The dove came back carrying an olive leaf, which was a sign of life on the land. So, the dove with an olive leaf became the symbol of peace. The word "dove" is also used in politics. A political "dove" is a politician whose ideas are mild, while a "hawk" is someone whose ideas are aggressive.

4 For those reasons, doves generally have a good image. They are prettier than pigeons and are associated with love and peace. Pigeons are generally considered to be a nuisance. The same thing can be said about ravens and crows, mice and rats, rabbits and hares etc. The first of each pair has a good image, and the others have a bad image.

1 それぞれの段落について、次の質問に答えなさい。

1. ピジョンとダブの言語学的違いは？

2. 日本の「ピジョン」という会社はなぜその名前をつけたのか？

3. アメリカの「ダブ」という会社はなぜその名前をつけたのか？

4. ピジョンとダブの区別は他のどんな動物にもあてはまるか？

2 If the statement refers to a pigeon, write P; and if it refers to a dove, write D.

(　　) 1. Its body color is grey.
(　　) 2. It is a symbol of peace.
(　　) 3. It was domesticated.
(　　) 4. Noah used it to see whether the land had life.
(　　) 5. Its name is given to a certain kind of politician.
(　　) 6. An American soap company uses its name.
(　　) 7. It was used as a messenger.
(　　) 8. Its name is used to mean a person who loses money in gambling.

3 A pigeon has a bad image and a dove has a good image. If the following word has a bad image, write P, and if a good image, write D.

(　　) raven
(　　) crow
(　　) mouse
(　　) rat
(　　) rabbit
(　　) hare

4 Write "T" if the statement is true and "F" if the statement is false.

(　　) 1. The word "dove" is from French.
(　　) 2. An aggressive politician is called a "pigeon politician."
(　　) 3. People generally love doves, but not pigeons.

Notes

[2] complain of ～の不満を言う　sign board 看板　domesticate 飼いならす　homing pigeon 伝書鳩　feeding bottle 哺乳瓶　[3] be linked to ～に関係している　corruption 腐敗・堕落　ark 船　release 放つ　flood 洪水　hawk タカ　aggressive 攻撃的な　[4] be associated with ～と関係がある　nuisance 迷惑

B Eastern and Western dragons

1 A dragon is a legendary creature that appears in the myths of many cultures. It looks like a snake, reptile and bird. There are two cultural dragon traditions: European dragons and Asian dragons.

2 In many Asian cultures, dragons are linked to a god or nature. They have some form of magic or other supernatural power. In some cultures, they can also speak. Most dragons are snake-like, with intelligence. They have four legs and are without wings. In Asia, dragons are respected and sometimes worshiped as gods.

3 In Europe, on the other hand, dragons are creatures to be challenged and killed by heroes. In the Bible, a snake tries to make Eve eat a forbidden apple, and it is said this snake might be the original dragon. In Europe, dragons existed before Christianity. Therefore, dragons were objects to be killed to show the power of Christianity.

4 Dragons may have developed differently in the West and in the East, but over the ages they may have interacted with each other. Nowadays, dragons are used in many computer games. The Japanese imaginary monster, Godzilla, might be a modern type of dragon.

上の文章の内容をまとめてみよう。

① 導入

② アジアのドラゴン

③ ヨーロッパのドラゴン

④ まとめ

Notes

1 legendary 伝説の　creature 生物　myth 神話　reptile とかげ　tradition 伝承
2 supernatural 超自然的な　intelligence 知性　worship 崇拝する　3 on the other hand 他方　challenge 挑む　hero 英雄　forbidden 禁断の　exist 存在する　Christianity キリスト教　object 対象物
4 interact with ～と相互作用する　imaginary 想像上の

Part II

6 For and Against
賛成と反対

エッセイ構成

❶ トピックの紹介
議論をよんでいる問題の紹介

❷ 賛成意見 ⇔ 対照 ⇔ ❸ 反対意見

❹ まとめ・コメント

現在議論をよんでいる問題をとりあげ、それに賛成する立場からの意見、それに反対する立場からの意見が紹介されます。

A Should Japan accept more foreigners?

1 Historically, the Japanese government has been reluctant to accept foreigners as workers and has limited the number of such workers. However, this attitude has been criticized both outside and inside Japan. To respond to such criticisms and to meet domestic economic needs, the Japanese government recently declared Japan would accept more foreign workers. Should we accept more foreigners as workers?

2 The supporters think that we should be more globalized. It's unfair to refuse people who want to work in Japan. Some people really want to live in Japan because their home country is politically or economically in danger. To refuse such people is inhumane. If we don't accept such people, it will lead to the death of many people. This is serious. Many people say if we live with foreign people, we can learn a lot from them. And more importantly, such foreign people may do the jobs Japanese people don't want to do.

3 People who are against this idea say that it will cause a lot of troubles. Foreign workers may take jobs from Japanese people. They are desperate, so they will do any work for low wages. Another problem is that if foreign workers are poor, the Japanese government has to spend money on them. If the government does not, there will be an increase in crime. We may have cultural troubles with them over environment, human relationships, noise, etc.

4 It will not be practical to refuse foreign workers, considering criticisms inside and outside Japan and our economic needs, so we should consider more seriously how to cooperate with foreign people.

1 それぞれの段落について、次の質問に答えなさい。

1. 外国人労働者に対する日本政府のこれまでの方針は？

____

2. 賛成の人たちは困っている外国人労働者を拒否することをどう思っているか？

____

3. 日本政府が貧しい外国人労働者を保護しないとどういうことが起こるか？

____

4. 筆者の意見をまとめよ。

____

2 Write "T" if the statement is true and "F" if the statement is false.

(　　) 1. The Japanese government has been tolerant to foreign workers throughout its history.

(　　) 2. Some people think that if we accept more foreigners they will be an economic burden.

(　　) 3. Everyone believes that Japan should accept foreigners who are suffering in their own country.

(　　) 4. There are some jobs no Japanese people want to do.

(　　) 5. Foreigners will do any job for low pay and take jobs from Japanese people.

3 Fill in the blanks to complete the summary.

Whether Japan should accept (1　　　　　) workers or not is discussed in this essay. The supporters think we should accept because we should be more (2　　　　　). The opponents think if we accept foreign workers, they will take (3　　　　　) from Japanese people and cause a lot of (4　　　　　). Such problems may cause more (5　　　　　).

4 Find the word in the text with the same meaning as the statement.

1. unwilling (　　　　　　)
2. to talk about somebody's faults or bad points (　　　　　　)
3. illegal activities or activities against law (　　　　　　)

Notes

1 be reluctant to V ～することをためらう　limit 制限する　attitude 態度　criticize 批判する　criticism 批判　meet ～ needs 必要を満たす　domestic 国内の　2 globalize グローバル化する　unfair 不公平な　refuse 拒絶する　inhumane 非人道的な　3 cause 引き起こす　desperate 切迫した　crime 犯罪　4 practical 現実的な　cooperate with ～と協力する

B Should St. Valentine's Day be abolished?

1 Nowadays giving and receiving chocolate on Saint Valentine's Day is a part of Japanese culture. Are you for or against this custom?

2 Some people think that St. Valentine's Day is good for the economy, because a lot of chocolate is sold for that day. More than half of chocolate consumed in Japan is sold during the month before St. Valentine's Day. Some people think it is a good chance to say "I love you" to somebody, because there are still many shy women in this country. It is also a good chance to say "thank you" to people around you at school or at work.

3 However, some people think we should abolish this custom. It is a waste of money. Usually men don't like chocolate so much. A lot of chocolate is thrown away or eaten reluctantly. There may be many women who think they have to give chocolate to everybody at work. For men, there is a problem, too. They are worried how many packages of chocolate they can get on the coming St. Valentine's Day.

4 We should consider the merits and demerits of St. Valentine's Day. What do you think?

上の文章の内容をまとめてみよう。

① 導入 → ② 賛成 → ③ 反対 → ④ まとめ

Notes

1 custom 慣習　2 consume 消費する　3 abolish 廃止する　waste 無駄　throw away 捨てる　reluctantly 嫌々　coming 来たる

Part II

7 Classification
分類してみよう！

エッセイ構成

ある基準を設け、その基準に従って、何かをいくつかのグループに分類するエッセイパターンです。どういう基準で分類されているのかに着目しましょう。

A Computer game genres

14

1 Children enjoyed various games in the past, such as cards, board games, hide-and-seek, etc. However, nowadays almost all children play computer games! How many computer games do you know? Here, let's try to classify computer games.

2 First, an "action game." It needs your physical movement and challenges. Most of the earliest video games were considered action games. The most famous one is Super Mario Brothers. Players guide a character through obstacles in order to get to the goal. Some shooting games and fighting games are also in this genre.

3 The second genre is an "adventure game." The player has to solve various puzzles by interacting with people or the environment. Adventure games do not put so much pressure on the player, so various people can enjoy them. Sometimes this genre includes an action game element. "The Legend of Zelda" by Nintendo includes puzzle solving, sword fighting, and item collecting.

4 The third genre is a "simulation game." The player plays it in a real or fictional setting. "SimCity" is an example. This game makes the player build a fictional city. There are business simulation games, which simulate an economy or business you have to control. A popular virtual pet, "Tamagotchi," is also an example of this genre. You have to take care of a virtual pet on the screen. This kind of game can be used for education, but there is also a love simulation game in which you choose your lover and can interact with him/her.

5 There are many other computer game genres, and this is a big market in Japan. Game creator is now one of the most popular jobs children want to have when they become adults.

Notes

1 hide-and-seek かくれんぼ　classify 分類する　2 physical 身体的な　guide 導く　character 登場人物　obstacle 障害　genre ジャンル　3 interact with ～　～と相互作用する　element 要素　sword 剣　item アイテム・品目　4 simulation 模擬　fictional setting 架空の設定　simulate 模する　virtual 仮想の

1 それぞれの段落について、次の質問に答えなさい。

1. 昔の子供の遊びの例を３つ挙げなさい。
   1. ______________________________
   2. ______________________________
   3. ______________________________
2. 「アクションゲーム」とは？

   ____

3. 「アドベンチャーゲーム」とは？

   ____

4. 「シミュレーションゲーム」とは？

   ____

5. コンピュータゲームは日本経済にどう影響しているか？

   ____

2 If the statement relates to "action games," write A; if it relates to "adventure games," write B; and if it relates to "simulation games," write C.

(　　) 1. Sim City.
(　　) 2. Tamagotchi
(　　) 3. The player has to go through many hardships and needs physical energy.
(　　) 4. Super Mario Brothers.
(　　) 5. The player needs to think to solve puzzles.
(　　) 6. A game to build a fictional city.
(　　) 7. A game in which you can love its characters.
(　　) 8. Shooting games.
(　　) 9. Most computer games started in this style.
(　　) 10. This type of game is very often used for education.

3 Write "T" if the statement is true and "F" if the statement is false.

(　　) 1. "The Legend of Zelda" is mentioned in this essay to show that it is a good example of a typical adventure game.
(　　) 2. An adventure game puts less pressure on a player than an action game.
(　　) 3. All computer games can be classified into these three genres.
(　　) 4. There is a business simulation game in which you can control an economy or business.

4 Find the word in the text with the same meaning as the statement.

1. a children's game in which one player shuts their eyes while the others hide, and then goes to look for them (　　　　　　　)
2. a person in a book, play, film etc. (　　　　　　　)
3. the activity of producing conditions which are similar to real ones (　　　　　　　)

B Thirdhand smoke

15

1 Smoking is bad not only for you but also for people around you. Do you know there are three types of smoke?

2 The "firsthand smoke" is the smoke that a smoker himself breathes in. If it harms the smoking person's health, it is his own responsibility.

3 The "secondhand smoke" is the smoke which people around the smoker breathe in. People who breathe in such smoke are also seriously affected. If you have a smoker in your family, or in your office, you are in danger.

4 The "thirdhand smoke" might be a new idea to you. It is the smoke which still exists in the air many hours after somebody has smoked. This pollution can last even hours after any visible smoke has disappeared. Toxic chemicals stay on the surfaces of the room, on the walls, on the windows, on the curtains, etc. If you stay in such a room, you will breathe in such toxic chemicals.

5 Even if you think your smoke affects only your own health, you might unconsciously damage other people's health.

上の文章の内容をまとめてみよう。

① 導入 → ② firsthand smoke → ③ secondhand smoke → ④ thirdhand smoke → ⑤ まとめ

Notes

thirdhand 二者を通しての
2 firsthand 直接的な　breathe in ～を吸い込む　harm 害する　responsibility 責任
3 secondhand 間接的な　seriously 深刻に　affect 影響を与える　be in danger 危険に陥っている
4 exist 存在する　pollution 汚染　last 続く　visible 目に見える　toxic 毒性の　chemical 化学物質
surface 表面　5 unconsciously 無意識的に

Part III

第３のパターン：直線型

（Unit 8 〜 10）

導入（トピックの提示）

第１段階

↓

第２段階

↓

第３段階

まとめ・これからの発展など

時間の流れに沿って順に説明をしていくものです。このテキストでは、⑧〜⑩課で次の３種類を提示します。

⑧ 歴史
⑨ 過程
⑩ 原因ー結果

Part III

8 History
歴史

エッセイ構成

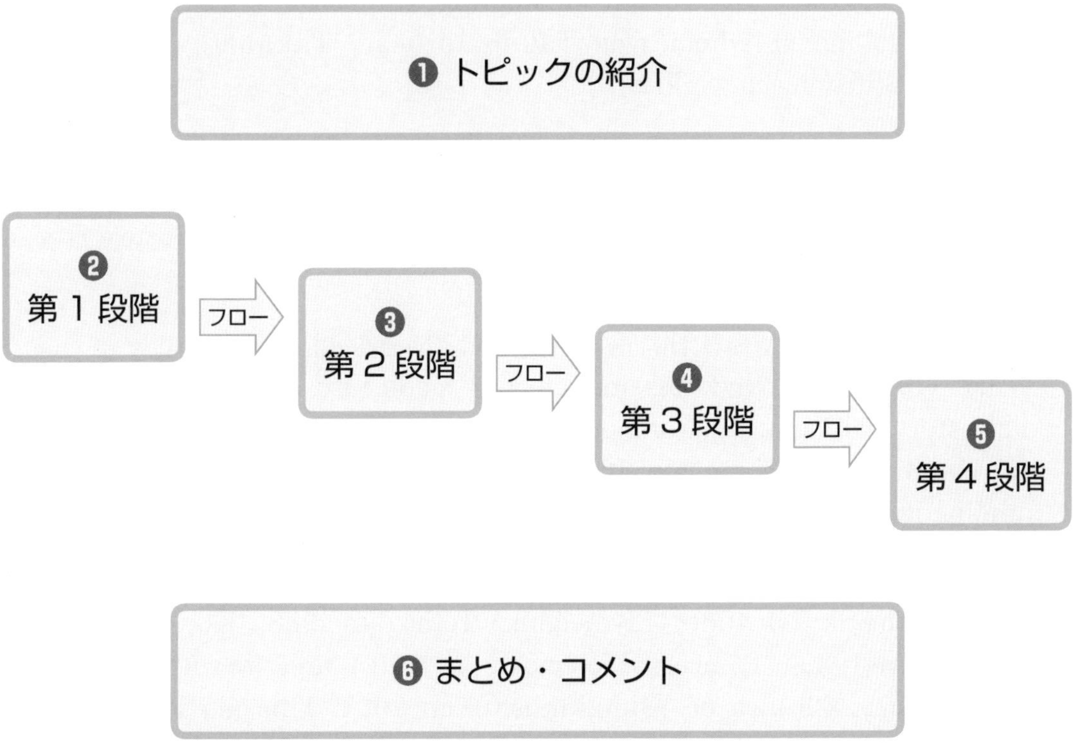

あるトピックについて、その時間的変遷を追っていくもの。まず何の歴史について説明するのかから始まり、時間的に早い内容から歴史をたどっていきます。最終段階として、現在の状態・状態で終わる。「まとめ」のパラグラフでは、現在の問題点、もしくは未来の予測などが述べられる。

A Miyazaki Hayao

1 Miyazaki Hayao is the most famous animation director in Japan, and has won several international awards.

2 Miyazaki was born in Tokyo in 1941. He lived through World War II, which later led him to make several war animation films. He was inspired by Tezuka Osamu and other cartoonists.

3 After graduating from Gakushuin University, he was employed at Toei Animation. He worked on making animation films with other animators, one of whom was Takahata Isao. Takahata would be Miyazaki's life-long co-worker.

4 In 1971, Miyazaki started to work for A-Pro. He co-directed "Lupin the Third" with Takahata. In 1973, he moved to Zuiyo Eizo with Takahata and worked on "Heidi, Girl of the Alps," and later "Future Boy Conan."

5 He started to draw the manga titled "Nausicaa of the Valley of the Wind" (1982-1994), and this manga was made into an animation film. This story criticizes environmental pollution. The film was released in 1984 and became a big hit. In 1984, Miyazaki opened his own office, naming it Nibariki.

6 Miyazaki built "Studio Ghibli" in 1985 and made the movie "Laputa: Castle in the Sky" in 1986, "My neighbor Totoro" in 1988, "Kiki's Delivery Service" in 1989, "Princess Mononoke" in 1997, and finally "Spirited Away (Sen to Chihiro no Kamikakushi)" in 2001. This movie won the Academy Award for Best Animated Feature at the 75th Academy Awards. He continued to make "Howl's Moving Castle" in 2004, and "Ponyo" in 2008.

7 In 2013 he announced his retirement, although he returned to work on a new film in 2016. In 2018, Takahata, Miyazaki's best partner, died.

1 それぞれの段落について、次の質問に答えなさい。

1. 宮崎駿の職業は？

____

2. 宮崎駿の作品に戦争を扱ったものがあるのはなぜ？

____

3. 高畑勲と宮崎駿をどういう関係か？

____

4. 高畑勲と製作したアニメを３つ挙げなさい。
   1. ______________________________________
   2. ______________________________________
   3. ______________________________________

5.「風の谷のナウシカ」はなにを批判していたか？

____

6. アカデミー賞で最優秀アニメーション賞をとった作品は？

____

7. 現在の状況は？

____

2 Fill in the blanks and complete the summary.

Miyazaki Hayao is a famous (1 　　　　　) director. His most successful work is "Spirited Away," which won an Academy (2 　　　　　) in 2001. He made many animated films with Takahata Isao, who was his (3 　　　　　) for life. "Nausicaa" is one of his successful works and it was made to criticize an (4 　　　　　) problem. He built his studio in 1985 and named it "Studio (5 　　　　　)." In this studio, he made many films. He (6 　　　　　) once, but he has come back to work again.

3 Write "T" if the statement is true and "F" if the statement is false.

(　　) 1. Miyazaki Hayao is working as a famous voice actor as well.
(　　) 2. Miyazaki was born just after World War II.
(　　) 3. Takahata Isao was Miyazaki's good co-worker and they made many works.
(　　) 4. Miyazaki's first office was named "Nibariki."
(　　) 5. "Ponyo" was made in Studio Ghibli in 2008.

Notes

1 director 監督　award 賞　2 live through 生き抜く・乗り越える　inspire 触発する　cartoonist 漫画家
3 employ 雇う　work on ～ ～に取り組む　life-long 生涯にわたっての　co-worker 共同制作者
4 co-direct 共同で製作する　5 criticize 批判する　environmental 環境の　pollution 汚染
release 発表する　6 neighbor 隣人　delivery 配達　spirited away 神隠し　7 announce 発表する
retirement 引退

B Tezuka Osamu

17

1 Tezuka Osamu was a pioneer of Japanese cartoons. He was an animator and almost everybody in Japan knows his works. His works include "Tetsuwan Atom (Astro Boy)," "Jungle Taitei Leo (Jungle Emperor)," and "Black Jack."

2 Tezuka was born in Osaka in 1928 and started to draw comics when he was a child, influenced by Walt Disney films. In 1945 he started to study medicine at the Osaka School of Medicine (now Osaka University). He used his knowledge of medicine later when making "Black Jack."

3 After graduating from the Osaka School of Medicine, he decided to become a cartoonist instead of a doctor. In 1952, Tetsuwan Atom began serialization in Shonen Magazine and became an instant hit in Japan.

4 In 1961, Tezuka started his animation work, founding "Mushi Productions." In 1962, his work "Tetsuwan Atom" was animated and became a hit. This was the first Japanese animation dubbed into English for an American audience. One after another, Tezuka's comics were made into animations. Some of them were introduced to other countries, giving them an international audience.

5 Tezuka died of stomach cancer in 1989. He was working on his comics until the end. Nobody would deny that he was the founder of the Japanese comic and animation culture.

上の文章の内容をまとめてみよう。

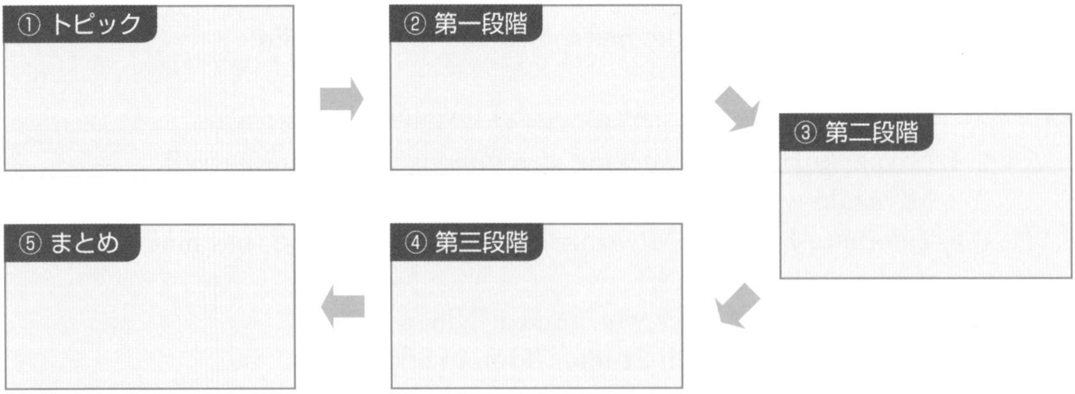

Notes

1 pioneer 開拓者　cartoon 漫画　animator アニメーション制作者　2 influence 影響を与える medicine 医学　knowledge 知識　3 serialization 連載　instant 即座の　4 found 創設する animate アニメにする　dub 吹き替えする　audience 観客　one after another 次から次へと make into ～に変える　5 stomach 胃　work on ～ ～に取りくむ　deny 否定する　founder 創始者

Part III

9 Processes
過程を説明する

エッセイ構成

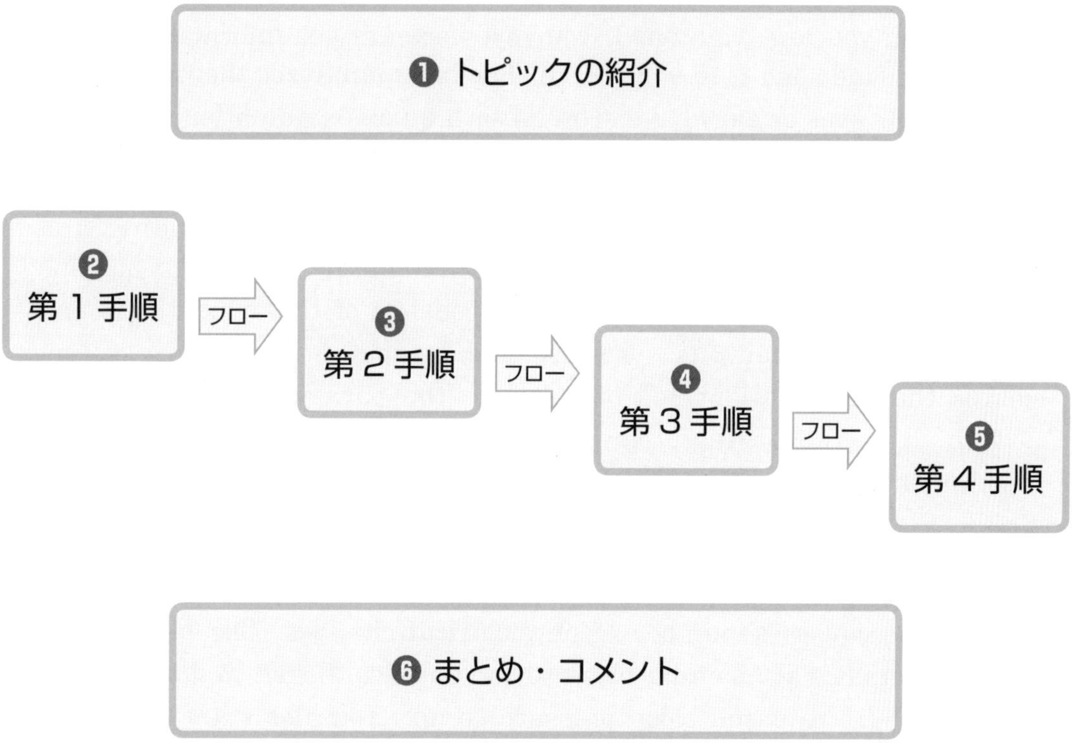

何かの過程を説明する。導入で何の過程を説明するのかを明示し、そのあとでその過程を説明していきます。「始めに→次に→それから→最後に」と進んでいくエッセイパターンです。

A How do you react to threats?

1 If you face a bear on the street, how do you react? Do you fight against or flee from it? You may be surprised at the strength you show in such a situation. This strength is called “fight-or-flight response” in English. Such a strength is a primitive survival mechanism animals including human beings inherently possess. To avoid danger, your body automatically responds to the crisis. How does your body react to a threat you are facing?

2 When you are frightened, your eyes or ears get information about the danger and send it to your brain. The brain analyzes the images and sounds your eyes or ears have sent. After a quick examination, the brain sends a distress signal to the hypothalamus.

3 The hypothalamus works like a command center, sending and receiving information to/from the body through the autonomic nervous system. The autonomic nervous system consists of the sympathetic and parasympathetic nervous systems. The sympathetic nervous system drives the fight-or-flight response, while the parasympathetic nervous system drives “freezing”. How you react depends on which system dominates the response at the time.

4 The hypothalamus sends signals to the adrenal glands. These glands send the hormone called adrenaline into the bloodstream. Adrenaline causes a number of physiological changes. The heart beats faster than normal, pushing blood to the muscles, heart, and other vital organs. Pulse rate and blood pressure go up. You also start to breathe more rapidly. Sight, hearing, and other senses become sharper. Such changes all concentrate your body’s energy to the vital organs to fight or flee.

5 This way, you may show an extraordinary strength which you have not expected. Sometimes you may freeze, not knowing what to do. In this case, the parasympathetic nervous system is stronger than the sympathetic nervous system.

1 それぞれの段落について、次の質問に答えなさい。

1. Fight-or-flight response を簡単に説明しなさい。

2. 目や耳が危険情報を得るとどうするか？

3. Hypothalamus（視床下部）はどういう働きをするか？

4. アドレナリンによる生理現象は何を目的としていますか？

5.「すくんでしまう」のは何が作用していますか？

2 Write "T" if the statement is true and "F" if the statement is false.

(　　) 1. To run away is more dangerous than fighting against your enemy.

(　　) 2. Human beings recently developed a fight-or-flight response when they meet an enemy.

(　　) 3. The hypothalamus receives the information from eyes or ears and then sends instructions to the body.

(　　) 4. The parasympathetic nervous system drives the fight-or-flight response.

(　　) 5. The adrenal glands release hormones and make you prepare to fight or flee.

3 Fill in the blanks to complete the sentence.

1. Your brain enters into ([1]) mode when you feel fear. This is a natural response for human beings.
2. The brain sends a distress signal to the ([2]).
3. The adrenal glands send the hormone which is called ([3]).
4. When your autonomic nervous system is stimulated, the heart rate and blood ([4]) go up.

Notes

react 反応する　threat 脅威　1 flee 逃げる　fight-or-flight response 戦うか逃げるか反応
primitive 原始的な　inherently 生まれつきの　possess 所有する　face 直面する　2 analyze 分析する
distress 苦痛　hypothalamus 視床下部　3 command 指令　autonomic nervous system 自律神経系統
consist of ～ ～から成っている　the sympathetic nervous system 交感神経系
the parasympathetic nervous system 副交感神経系　drive 操る・引き起こす　freezing すくみ
dominate 支配する　4 the adrenal gland 副腎　hormone ホルモン　adrenaline アドレナリン
bloodstream 血流　physiological 生理的な　muscle 筋肉　vital 重要な　organ 器官
concentrate 集中させる　5 extraordinary 異常な　freeze 凍りつく

B How does memory tell lies?

19

1 How reliable are eyewitnesses? Eyewitnesses make mistakes even though they think they are telling the truth. This essay explains how your memory tells a lie.

2 First, an eyewitness has to recognize what he has seen. When he sees an unexpected event, there is often confusion and fear. According to studies, the brain recognizes only the main part of the scene and does not recognize details.

3 Second, an eyewitness has to form the memory. However, there are lots of gaps in his memory, because he has not recognized details of the scene. The brain doesn't like gaps, so these gaps are often filled with something that is not reliable. This can result in false memories.

4 Finally, we have to take out the memory. Every time we tell a false memory to another person, we tend to strengthen the false memory. In the end the eyewitness believes he is telling what he has seen.

5 Since the start of DNA testing in the 1990s, hundreds of innocent Americans have been released. About 75% of those people were arrested because of mistaken eyewitness stories.

上の文章の内容をまとめてみよう。

① 導入 → ② 第一段階 → ③ 第二段階 → ④ 第三段階 → ⑤ まとめ

Notes

1 reliable 信頼できる　eyewitness 目撃者　2 unexpected 予期せぬ　confusion 混乱　scene 場面・シーン　3 form 形づくる　result in ～という結果になる　false 誤った　4 take out 取り出す　strengthen 強化する　in the end 最後には　5 innocent 無実の　release 釈放する　arrest 逮捕する

Part III

10 Causes & Effects
原因から結果へ

エッセイ構成

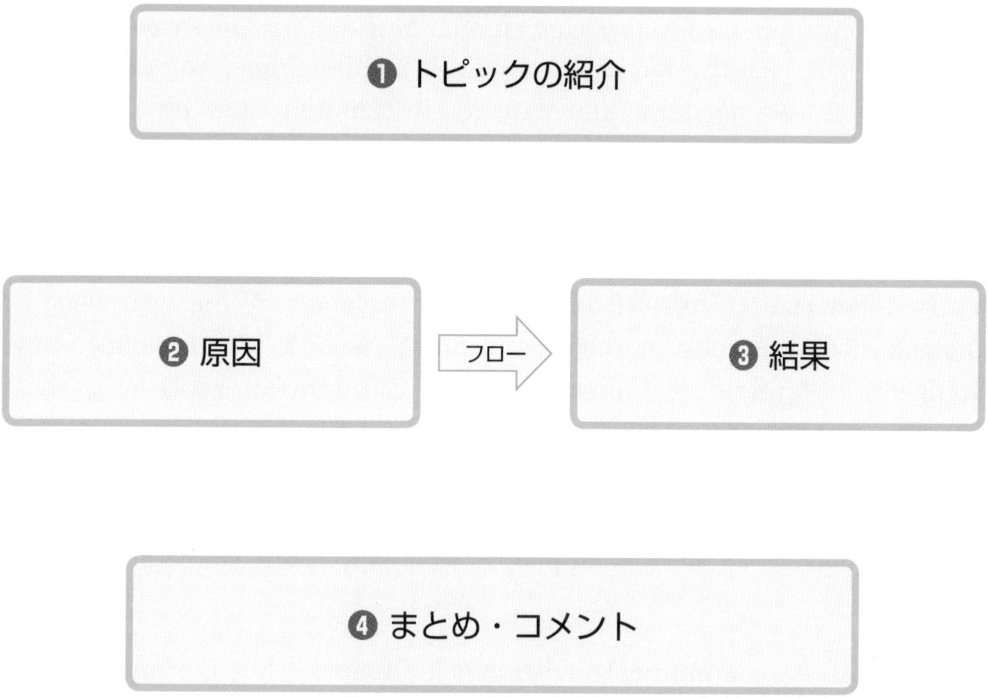

ボディとなるパラグラフが、原因 → その結果、と進むエッセイパターン。何かの事象があり、それが原因となってあることが起こる、その過程がこのエッセイでは述べられる。第 3 課の結果 ← 原因のエッセイとは対をなすものである。

A What did we lose with mobile phones?

1 If you are lost on the street, you can ask your mobile phone where you are and where your destination is. Your mobile phone tells you which train you should use, at which station you should change, and how long it takes to get to your destination. This way, the mobile phone saves us space, time and energy. Nowadays mobile phones are necessary in our daily life. Almost everybody, except for older people and very young children, has a mobile phone.

2 A mobile phone is very convenient. You don't need to carry many things in your bag any more if you have a mobile phone. You can contact people when you need to. You can get information just by pressing a button. Thanks to mobile phones, life has become very comfortable.

3 However, you should consider what you have lost because of mobile phones. First, now that your mobile phone knows everything, you don't try to memorize things, think, or solve problems. What you need to know is just which button you should press. Second, mobile phones have changed our human relationships. People communicate with only those who they want to. You don't need to communicate with the people around you. You can contact people who have the same interests and opinions as you, and you can refuse to communicate with other people, although you could learn a lot from such people, and as a result your views will be biased.

4 It's nice to communicate with people far away, but is it good to lose contact with people around you or people who have different views from you?

1 それぞれの段落について、次の質問に答えなさい。

1. 携帯電話をあまり使わない二つの層とは？

____

2. ここで挙げられている携帯電話の利点を三つ挙げなさい。

 1. ______________________________
 2. ______________________________
 3. ______________________________

3. 携帯電話のせいで私たちが失ったものを２つ挙げなさい。

 1. ______________________________
 2. ______________________________

4. 筆者が投げかけている疑問とは？

____

2 Write "T" if the statement is true and "F" if the statement is false.

( ) 1. Most older people use mobile phones because they are necessary in their daily life.

( ) 2. All you have to do to get information is press a button on your mobile phone.

( ) 3. You don't have to solve problems by yourself because your mobile phone does it for you.

( ) 4. It is a good thing to talk with people who have different opinions from you.

3 Fill in the blanks to complete the following summary.

A mobile phone is now (1) in our daily life and everyone always carries one to save space in their (2), to contact people and to get (3). On the other hand, we have lost some important things. We can't (4) things because our mobile phone memorizes everything. We have lost many human (5) by refusing (6) with people who we don't like.

4 Find the word in the text with the same meaning as the statement.

1. not fixed in one position, and easy to move and use in different places
 (m)
2. a small part of a machine that you press to make it do something
 (b)

Notes

2 contact 連絡する　3 button ボタン　press 押す　view 考え方　be biased 偏見をもっている

B Some jobs are disappearing with the spread of computers

21

1 We now live in a computer society, and everybody is now connected through the Internet and can get any information whenever and wherever they want.

2 The computer has completely changed our lifestyles. The most important change is that we can share information equally wherever we live. Through the Internet we can participate in the activities all around the world, and we can receive and give information.

3 However, nowadays many people are afraid of losing their jobs because of computers. First, bookshops are disappearing. Almost all books are available online, and we read them on the computer screen. Second, we don't need cinemas anymore because we can watch movies on the Internet. Third, photo shops are disappearing because you can keep your photos on your computer. Thanks to mobile phones and digital cameras combined with a computer, people can edit and print photos easily.

4 These are just some examples. It is sad to see familiar shops disappearing. These shops have to find new ways to cope with computers.

上の文章の内容をまとめてみよう。

① 導入

② 原因

③ 結果

④ まとめ

Notes

2 equally 平等に participate in ～に参加する combine with ～と組み合わせる edit 編集する

3 be available 手に入る digital デジタルの

4 familiar おなじみの cope with ～と協力する

Part IV

第４のパターン：異質パラグラフ型

（Unit 11 ～ 14）

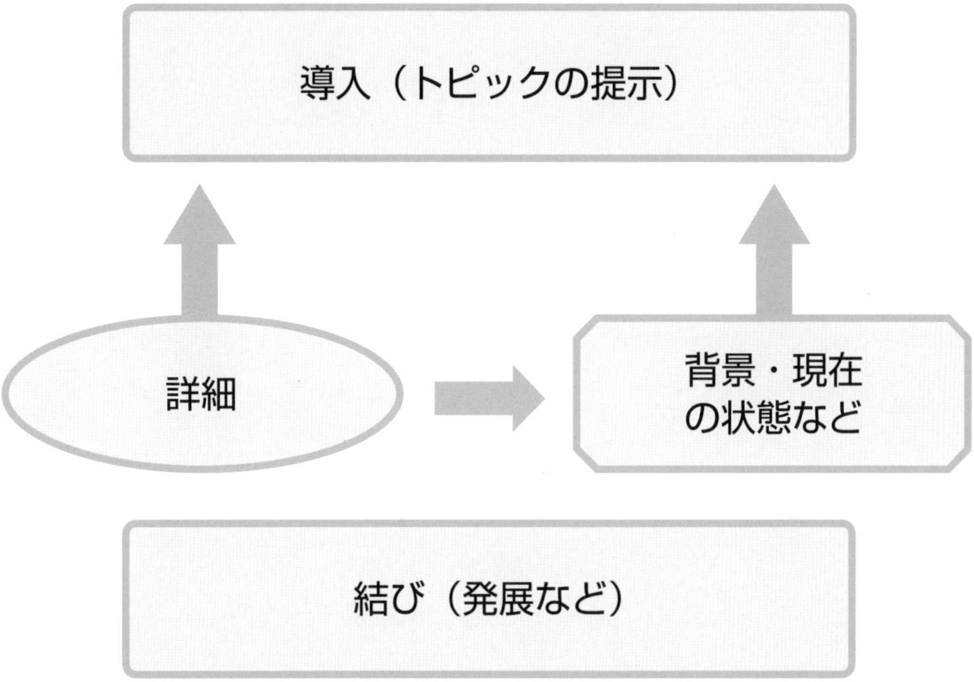

役割の違う複数のパラグラフで構成するエッセイパターンです。このテキストでは⑪～⑭課で次の４種類を提示します。

⑪ 問題解決
⑫ 言葉の定義
⑬ 実験
⑭ 新製品

Part IV

11 Definition of New Words
最近気になる言葉を考えよう

エッセイ構成：マルチ展開型

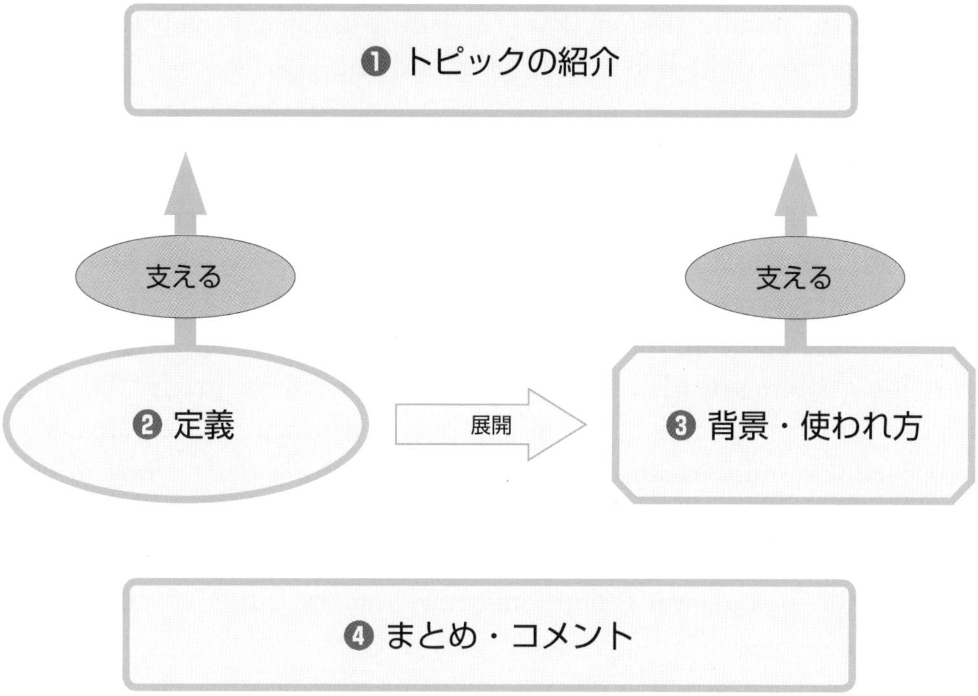

テレビ・雑誌・新聞などで最近よく聞く・見る新しい言葉を考察するエッセイです。もともとはどういう意味なのか、その元来の意味を基にして、現在はどのように使われているのか、なぜその言葉が流行っているのかが述べられます。

A School castes

1 Bullying has always existed in school society. It has shown various forms through history, and now a new type of bullying has appeared.

2 The phrase “school caste” is new and it has been spreading through the Internet. As you know, the word “caste” means a social system which has existed in India for a long time. There are four main statuses in the caste system: priests, kings and nobles, common people, and slaves. Schools have a similar system to Indian castes. The ruling group has the power and the middle group follows the ruling group. At the bottom, there is the lower group which is the target of bullying.

3 There has been always such a hierarchy in schools. However, there is a difference between the traditional order and school castes: the ruling group differs from other people because they have high communication skills. In the past, the ruling group had physical or academic skills. Students who were good at sports or fighting, or were clever, were respected and made up the ruling group. However, nowadays the students with high communication skills make up the ruling group. They can use the Internet to make a group and decide who will be excluded. They spread rumors online. Nowadays people who have more friends in class or through the Internet are respected and have power. To make matters worse, such castes sometimes change. A member in the ruling group today can be in the lower group tomorrow, and the target of bullying and vice versa.

4 School castes are a new form of social order. This is very often invisible to teachers and parents and they hardly recognize what is going on in school. To solve this problem, it is important to find out how it is working in school as soon as possible.

1 それぞれの段落について、次の質問に答えなさい。

1. 歴史を通じていじめはどのような形態をとってきたか？

____

2. 現代のクラスにおける支配階級、中層階級、下層階級の関係性を説明しなさい。

____

3. スクールカーストが従来のクラス内での階層と違っているのはどういう点か？

____

4. スクールカースト問題を解決するにはどうしたらいいか？

____

2 If the statement is about the traditional order at school, write T; and if it is about the new "school caste" system, write S.

(　　) 1. The ruling group has high communication skills.
(　　) 2. The ruling group has physical skills.
(　　) 3. The ruling group has academic skills.
(　　) 4. Students who are good at any sport are respected.
(　　) 5. Students who can use the Internet effectively are respected.
(　　) 6. Students who have many friends make up the ruling group.
(　　) 7. To bully a target student, the ruling group spreads rumors online.

3 Fill in the blanks to complete the summary.

Targets of (1　　　　　　　　) at school have always been a part of Japanese society. Bullying was done by the students who were good at (2　　　　　　　　), fighting, or studying. However, nowadays a new order has appeared at school, called "(3　　　　　　　　) castes." Under this order, the students who can (4　　　　　　　　) with people well and can use the (5　　　　　　　　) well make up the ruling group.

4 Find the word in the text with the same meaning as the statement.

1. threatening to hurt or frighten someone, especially someone smaller or weaker (　　　　　　)
2. someone who is specially trained to perform religious duties and ceremonies (　　　　　　)
3. information or a story that is passed from one person to another (　　　　　　)

Notes

caste カースト（制）　[1] bullying いじめ　[2] status 地位・階層　priest 僧侶　noble 貴族　slave 奴隷　similar 同様の　ruling 支配的な　target 標的　[3] hierarchy 階層（制度）　academic 学術的な・勉強　make up ～を形成する　exclude 排除する　rumor 噂　to make matters worse さらに悪いことには　vice versa その反対　[4] social order 社会階層・社会秩序

B Charaben

1 Fancy "obento" or boxed lunches are now popular among foreign people as well. They are considered part of Japanese culture.

2 "Charaben" is a word which combines two words, "character" and "bento." The word started to be used around 2000 and many books have been published with photos of charaben. Mothers enjoy making fancy bento, by cutting and cooking food in the shape of anime characters. The original type of character food was an octopus-shaped sausage or a rabbit shaped apple slice. Such skills developed into a kind of artistic "charaben."

3 Why do mothers make such fancy obento? First, mothers, especially housewives, have time and money. The media puts pressure on mothers to be good mothers. Some mothers don't like this trend, but some mothers find their own pleasure in making a beautiful obento as a hobby. They have a good place to show the lunches they make: the Internet. They show their own works on their blog, or on Facebook.

4 Nowadays many foreign people have joined charaben circles on the Internet.

上の文章の内容をまとめてみよう。

① 導入

② 言葉の定義

③ 背景

④ まとめ

Notes

1 boxed 箱詰めの　2 combine 結びつける　publish 出版する　fancy きれいな
in the shape of ～の形に　original 原型の　octopus タコ　artistic 芸術的な
3 put pressure on A to V Aが～するように圧力をかける

12 Research
調査をしよう

エッセイ構成：マルチ展開型

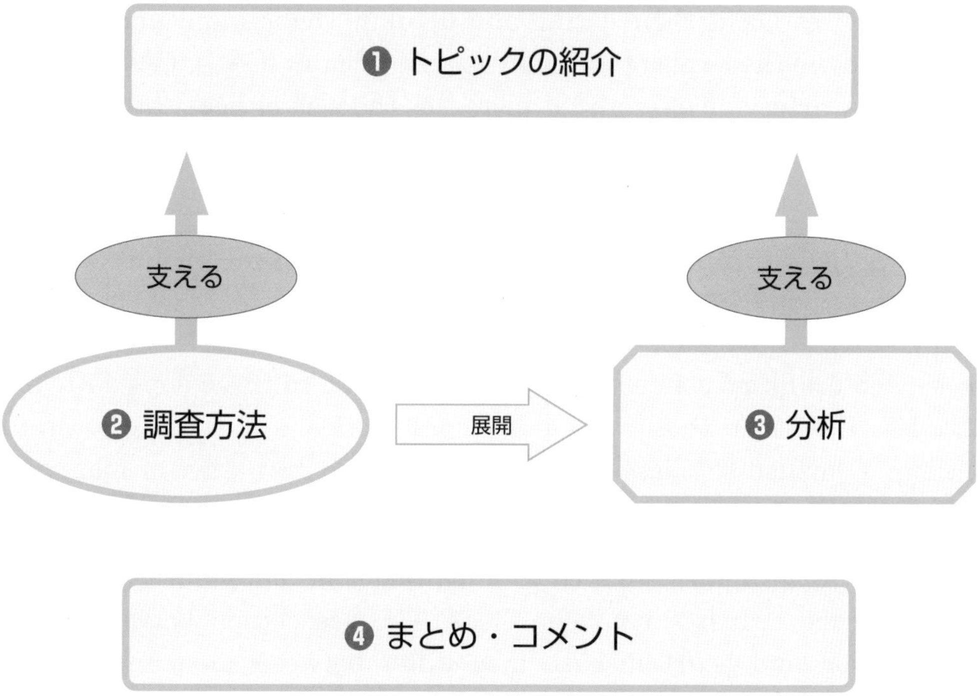

ある調査が紹介され、その結果や、その調査から言えること、なぜそういう結果になったのかの説明がされるエッセイパターンです。

A Coffee reduces the risk of heart disease

24

1 How many cups of coffee do you drink a day? None or as many as five cups? Is it good for your health or not? Professor Guallar and his colleagues at the Kangbuk Samsung Hospital in Seoul studied the relationship between coffee and heart diseases, using 25,000 men and women. This research was conducted between 2013 and 2015.

2 The participants had no signs of heart disease and their average age was 41 at the start of the study. The participants answered questionnaires about their eating and drinking habits and underwent a CT scan to see the levels of coronary artery calcium (CAC). CAC is a sign of coronary artery disease and it increases the risk of heart attacks. The researchers compared people's CAC levels with the amount of coffee they drink.

3 This is the result of the research. The average amount was 1.8 cups per day, and 13.4% of all the participants had CAC. The people who drank three to five cups of coffee daily had about 40% less CAC than those who drank no coffee. Those who drank one to three cups daily had 35% less CAC than those who didn't drink coffee, and those who drank one cup a day had 23% less CAC. The people who drank five or more cups a day had 19% less CAC, compared with those who drank no coffee.

4 The researchers say that a connection between coffee and heart disease risk has not been clear. The association between coffee consumption and heart disease may differ between men and women. However, they say if there is a connection, it may be due to the antioxidants that coffee contains. And according to the research, three to five cups of coffee per day may be the best amount.

1 それぞれの段落について、次の質問に答えなさい。

1. Guallar 教授たちは何を調べたか？

____

2. CAC とは何か？

____

3. 調査結果からどんなことがわかったか？

____

4. 科学者はコーヒーが心臓病に効く理由として何を挙げているか？

____

2 Fill in the blanks with numbers.

1. (　　　　　) people were used in research by Professor Guallar and his colleagues.
2. The average age of the participants in this research was (　　　　　) when the research started.
3. According to the research results, the average amount of coffee the participants drank was (　　　　　) cups per day.
4. According to the research results, (　　　　　) percent of all the participants had CAC.
5. The people who drank three to five cups of coffee a day had (　　　　　) percent less CAC than those who drank no coffee.

3 Fill in the blanks to complete the summary.

The team at the Kangbuk Samsung Hospital conducted research to find the relationship between ([1] 　　　　　) and heart diseases. They asked 25,000 people to participate in the research. The participants didn't have any ([2] 　　　　　) disease and their average ([3] 　　　　　) was 41. CAC is a ([4] 　　　　　) of coronary artery disease which causes a heart attack. The participants had to undergo CT ([5] 　　　　　) to see the level of CAC. According to the research results, the amount of ([6] 　　　　　) they drank was linked to the ([7] 　　　　　) of heart diseases.

4 Find the word in the text with the same meaning as the statement.

1. someone who is taking part in an activity or event (　　　　　)
2. a written set of questions which you give to many people in order to collect information (　　　　　)
3. a silver-white metal that helps to form teeth, bones, and chalk (　　　　　)

Notes

1 colleague 同僚　Seoul ソウル　2 participant 被験者　sign 兆候　questionnaire アンケート　undergo 受ける　coronary artery 動脈　heart attack 心筋梗塞　compare A with B　A を B と比較する
4 connection 関係　antioxidant 抗酸化物質

B What kind of music do fetuses like?

1 A Spanish research team examined whether a fetus responds to music or not.

2 They used a special speaker to make fetuses listen to different types of music. They tested 300 fetuses between 18 and 38 weeks old. While the fetuses listened, the researchers watched their mouth and tongue movements on an ultrasound machine.

3 The fetuses responded more to classical music than to pop or rock. 91% of the babies showed mouth movements, and 73% stuck out their tongue when they listened to Mozart's "A Little Night Music." When they listened to "Bohemian Rhapsody" by Queen, 90% of babies moved their mouths, but only 40% stuck out their tongue. Songs by Adele, the Bee Gees and Shakira impressed 60% or less of the fetuses.

4 You should choose the type of music for your baby.

上の文章の内容をまとめてみよう。

① 導入

② 調査の説明

③ 調査の結果

④ まとめ・結論

Notes

fetus 胎児　1 examine 調べる　whether ～かどうか　respond 反応する　2 ultrasound 超音波
3 stick out 突き出す　impress 印象づける

13 New Products
新製品

エッセイ構成：マルチ展開型

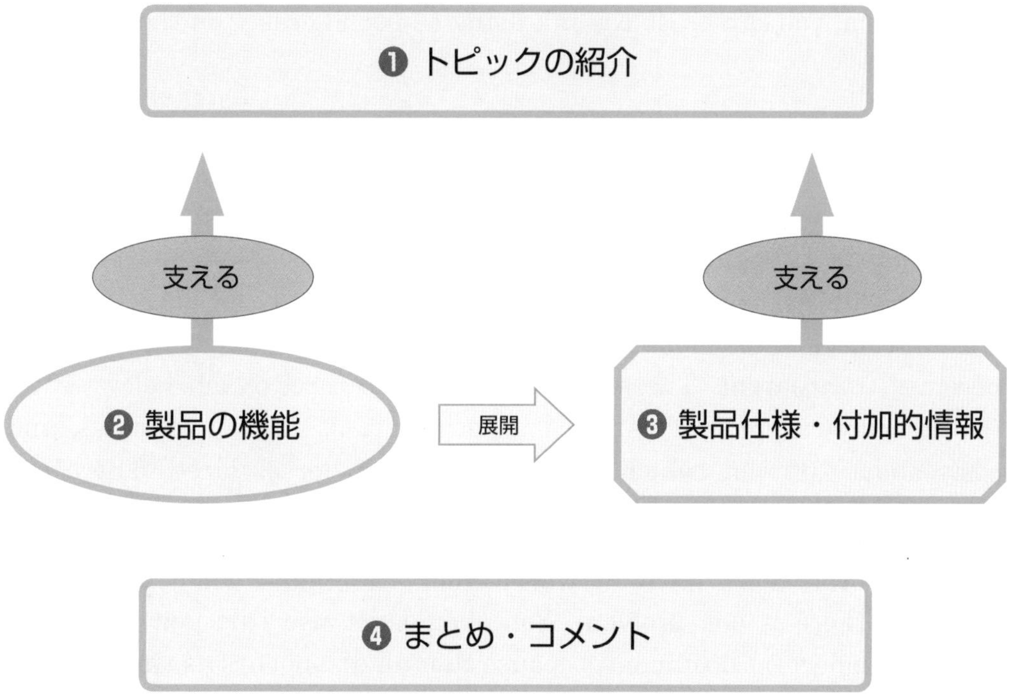

新製品のプロモーション・エッセイです。製品の特徴を紹介し、その製品がどんな点で新しいのか、どういうところで役に立つのかといったことが述べられ、もう一つのパラグラフではその製品の形・色・サイズ・値段などの詳細が述べられます。

A FriXion pens

1 Pilot's "FriXion Ball" is a unique ballpoint pen. You may have one already. This pen was invented and developed by Pilot, a Japanese stationery company, and now it is popular outside Japan, too.

2 With no damage to the paper, you can erase and instantly rewrite over your mistakes. This pen has a ballpoint tip at one end and a plastic-like eraser at the other end. In the past, when you wrote something on paper with a ballpoint pen, you could not erase it. However, with a FriXion pen, you can erase the ink using a special eraser on the tip of the pen.

3 The secret behind the magic is in a special ink. The ink contains three types of special microcapsules. A is the color pigment, B is the color-activating component, and C is what makes the color transparent when it is heated. At regular temperatures, A and B are combined, and the color appears. When you rub the ink with a special eraser, heat from the friction causes A to combine with C so that B is ineffective, and the ink becomes transparent. Therefore, when temperatures reach below -10℃, the ink may reappear. This pen is sold in various colors and styles, and costs about 200 yen, which is reasonable even for children. There are pens with 0.38, 0.4, 0.5 and 0.7 mm tips.

4 Now you don't have to worry about mistakes when you write. However, there is one problem. You should not use this pen when you write an important document, because the ink disappears as time passes.

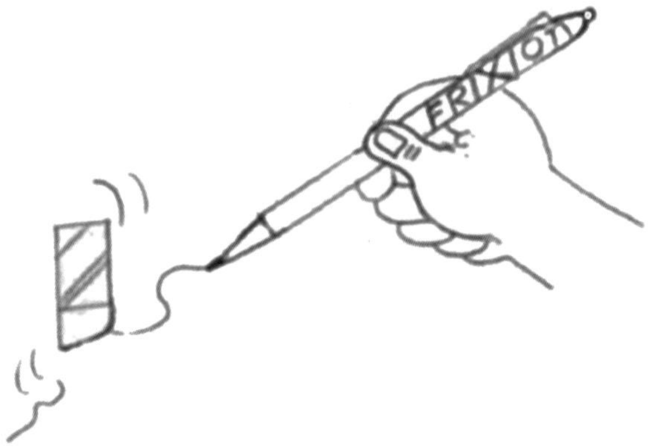

1 それぞれの段落について、次の質問に答えなさい。

1.「フリクション・ボール」を開発したのは誰か？

____

2.「フリクション・ボール」はなぜ注目されているのか？

____

3. インクに含まれる A, B, C のマイクロカプセルはどのような特徴をもっているか？

A. ______________________________

B. ______________________________

C. ______________________________

4.「フリクション・ボール」を使う上での問題点

____

2 Put the following statements in the right order.

1. The color appears with the help of the color-activating component in the ink.
2. A special microcapsule in the ink is combined with the pigment and it makes the ink transparent.
3. You can rewrite after your mistake has become transparent.
4. The ink is heated when you rub with a special eraser on the tip of the pen.
5. You write something on the paper with a FriXion pen.

(　　) → (　　) → (　　) → (　　) → (　　)

3 Fill in the blanks to complete the following summary.

The "FriXion Ball" pen developed by (1 　　　　　　), a Japanese company, is unique, because you can instantly rewrite over your (2 　　　　　　) even though they are written with a (3 　　　　　　) pen. This pen has a special (4 　　　　　　) on the tip of the pen. When you make mistakes, you can (5 　　　　　　) the mistakes on the paper with this special eraser. Special microcapsules in the ink make the color (6 　　　　　　). This is very convenient, but don't use this pen when you write an important (7 　　　　　　) because the ink disappears as (8 　　　　　　) passes.

4 Write "T" if the statement is true and "F" if the statement is false.

(　　) 1. "FriXion Ball" is a kind of pencil with a special power.

(　　) 2. There are three types of special microcapsules in the ink and all these three make the ink disappear.

(　　) 3. The price of a "FriXion Ball" is reasonable, so even children can buy one.

(　　) 4. When you rub the ink with the special eraser, you cause the ink to heat up.

Notes

1 unique 独特な・ユニークな　ballpoint pen ボールペン　2 instantly すぐに　rewrite 書き直す　end 端　tip 先端　3 microcapsule マイクロカプセル　pigment 顔料　color-activating component 色を出現させる成分　transparent 透明の　rub こする　friction 摩擦　cause A to V Aが～するようにさせる　ineffective 機能しない　reasonable 安価な

B Robot hotel

1 Maybe you expect warm hospitality when you stay at a hotel. However, if you hear that such hospitality is provided by robots, how do you feel?

2 A hotel called "Hen-na Hotel" ("Strange Hotel") has opened next to Huis Ten Bosch, a famous theme park in Nagasaki. The staff of this hotel are mainly androids that work as receptionists, waiters, cleaning staff, etc. They look like young women, men, or sometimes dinosaurs (to amuse children). These robots can speak several languages.

3 Why was such a hotel developed? This hotel is a part of Huis Ten Bosch, a theme park. As a part of a theme park, you can enjoy communicating with robots. You can see how much robots can do instead of humans. Of course, this kind of hotel can save staff costs and makes the room rate lower. Room rates start at about $60 US (7,000 yen).

4 If you want to stay at a low-price hotel, and you want something to talk about with your friends, why don't you try "Hen-na Hotel"?

上の文章の内容をまとめてみよう。

① 導入 → ② サービスの内容 → ③ 背景 → ④ まとめ

Notes

1 hospitality もてなし　2 Huis Ten Bosch ハウステンボス　a theme park テーマパーク　staff 従業員　android アンドロイド　receptionist 受付　dinosaur 恐竜　amuse 楽しませる　3 room rate 宿泊料

Part IV

14 Reading Graphs
グラフを読む

エッセイ構成：マルチ展開型

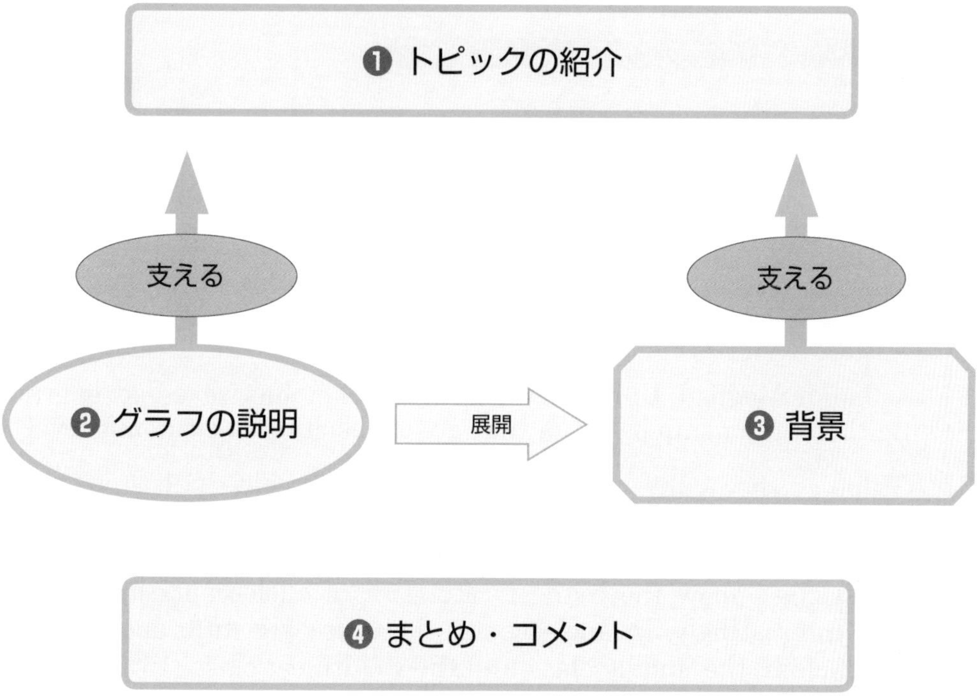

調査のレポート、プレゼンテーションなどで、グラフはよく使われます。グラフをまず説明し、どのようなことがグラフからわかるのか、なぜこのような結果になったのかの分析や推測が述べられます。

The following graph is linked to the essay below.

Graph A : obesity rates in adolescents

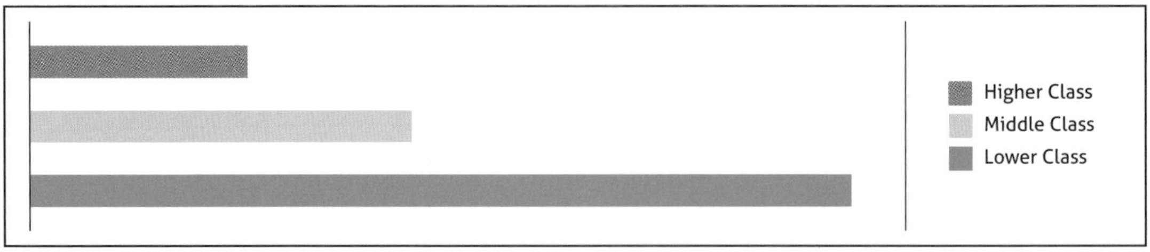

Graph B: obesity rates in children

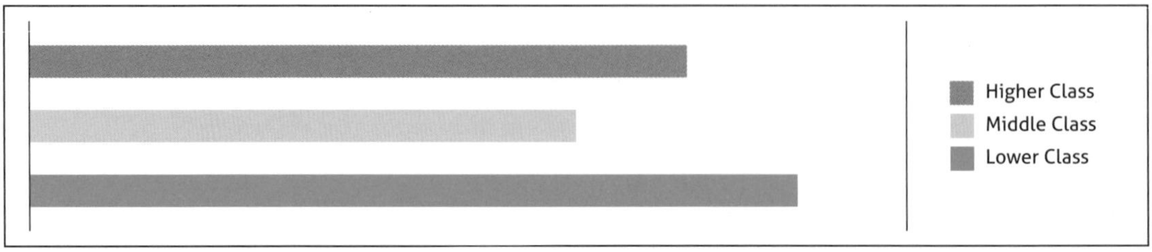

A Poverty brings obesity

1 A Japan Medical University research team has revealed a graph showing the relationship between the rate of obesity and economic level.

2 Graph A shows the rate of obesity in adolescents (12 to 18 years old) according to the economic level of their family. Graph B shows the rate of obesity in children (6 to 11 years old). In both graphs, people from the poorest class show the highest rate (15% of adolescents and 14% of children). Interestingly, in adolescents, there are big differences among the poorest class, the middle class and the wealthiest class (15%, 7%, and 4% respectively), while in children, there is not such a big difference (14%, 10%, and 12% respectively).

3 Why are children from the poorest class overweight? The reason is that they eat inexpensive but high calorie foods, for example, fast food, food high in carbohydrates etc. Their parents are both at work and have no time to cook for their children. Middle-class and wealthier mothers tend to be more health-conscious and they have the time and money to cook for their children. However, in childhood, there is not such a big gap among the three classes. Why? The answer may be in Japan's school meal system. Children can have school meals at school. This fact may explain the narrower gap among the economic classes.

4 It is usually thought that rich people suffer from obesity, but in reality, poor people suffer more from obesity.

1 それぞれの段落について、次の質問に答えなさい。

1. このグラフは何を示しているか？

____

2. A のグラフと B のグラフは何を示しているか？

A. ______________________________

B. ______________________________

3. なぜ下層階級の子供たちが肥満なのか？

____

4. 肥満と経済レベルの関係が示す矛盾点とは？

____

2 Write "T" if the statement is true and "F" if the statement is false.

(　　) 1. People from the poorest class have the highest rate in both Graph A and Graph B.

(　　) 2. The difference between the three classes is bigger for adolescents than for children.

(　　) 3. Children from the poorest class tend to have parents who work.

(　　) 4. Middle and wealthiest class mothers tend to be more interested in health.

(　　) 5. The difference between classes is smaller in childhood because children learn the importance of food at school.

3 Fill in the blanks with numbers.

1. Adolescents in this research means people from (　　　　　) to 18 years old.
2. The rate of obesity in middle-class children is (　　　　　) percent.

4 Answer the following questions in English.

1. Why is there a smaller gap in obesity rates between the three classes in children compared to adolescents?

____

2. What is a good example of high calorie food?

____

Notes

poverty 貧困　obesity 肥満　1 reveal 公表する　2 rate 率　adolescent 青年期の若者
3 overweight 太り過ぎの　inexpensive 高価ではない　calorie カロリー　carbohydrate 炭水化物
conscious 意識した

B The number of students who go abroad to study has been declining in Japan.

1 The following graph shows the number of Japanese students who went abroad to study from 1983 to 2010.

2 The number rises constantly from 1983 to a peak in 2004. And then the number starts to decline and continues to fall until 2010.

3 Why are fewer and fewer Japanese people going abroad to study? The first reason is that nowadays it is possible to learn English or other languages at home. People can learn foreign languages easily on the Internet. The second reason is that people feel comfortable in their home country. They can get whatever they want from foreign countries on the Internet.

4 It is good that everybody has a chance to learn about foreign cultures on the Internet, whether he is rich or not. However, the trend that young people avoid adventures might be dangerous for our society. Experiences of different cultures can teach young people a lot of things.

上の文章の内容をまとめてみよう。

① 導入

② グラフの説明

③ 背景

④ まとめ

Notes

decline 減少する　2 constantly 継続して　peak ピーク　4 trend 傾向　avoid 避ける

■ Change in the number of people who go abroad to study

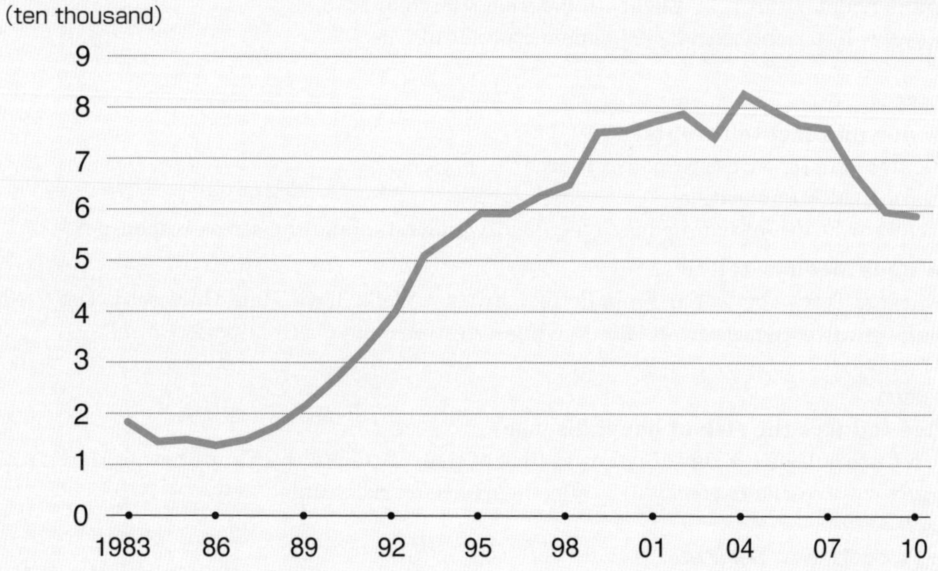

参照

4. Several Explanations

Acupuncture

"What is Acupuncture?" by Elizabeth Palermo, March 5, 2015
http://www.livescience.com/29494-acupuncture.html

9. Processes

How do you react to threats?

Understanding the stress response, March 2011
Harvard Health Publication
https://www.health.harvard.edu/staying-healty/understanding-the-stress-response

How does memory tell lies?

Eyewitness Testimony is Far From Perfect, by Gary Wells, Iowa State University, Dec.01, 2014
https://www.livescience.com/48966-eyewitness-testimony-is-far-from-perfect.html

12. Research

Coffee reduces the risk of heart disease

"3 to 5 Cups of Coffee a Day May Lower Risk of Heart Attacks," by Tanya Lewis, March 2, 2015.
https://www.livescience.com/50012-coffee-heart-attack-risk.html

13. New Products, New Services

Robot hotel

"World's First Robot-Staffed Hotel to Open in Japan", by Tanya Lewis, February 05, 2015
https://www.livescience.com/49711-japanese-robot-hotel.html

14. Reading Graphs

Poverty brings obesity

Nihon Keizai Shinbun Aug. 10, 2015
日本から海外への留学者数の推移
文部科学省

Skills for Better Reading <Intermediate> —Third Edition—

構造で読む英文エッセイ〈中級編〉【第３版】 [B-926]

１刷　2021 年 2 月 16 日
２刷　2022 年 9 月 28 日

著　者　石谷　由美子　Yumiko Ishitani

発行者　南雲一範　Kazunori Nagumo
発行所　株式会社　南雲堂
〒 162-0801　東京都新宿区山吹町 361
NAN'UN-DO Co., Ltd.
361 Yamabuki-cho, Shinjuku-ku, Tokyo 162-0801, Japan
振替口座：00160-0-46863
TEL: 03-3268-2311（営業部：学校関係）
03-3268-2384（営業部：書店関係）
03-3268-2387（編集部）
FAX: 03-3269-2486

編集者　加藤　敦
イラスト　さとう　有作
装　丁　N スタジオ
組　版　Office haru
検　印　省　略
コード　ISBN978-4-523-17926-9　C0082

Printed in Japan

E-mail nanundo@post.email.ne.jp
URL https://www.nanun-do.co.jp/